T0128778

# PLAY THE CRAPS GAME— THE RIGHT WAY

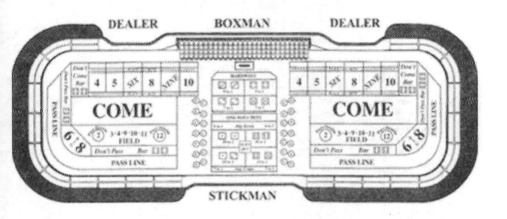

## WALLACE CHIN

authorHOUSE®

*AuthorHouse™*
*1663 Liberty Drive*
*Bloomington, IN 47403*
*www.authorhouse.com*
*Phone: 1-800-839-8640*

*Published by AuthorHouse 8/21/2012*

*ISBN: 978-1-4772-4947-5 (sc)*
*ISBN: 978-1-4772-4948-2 (hc)*
*ISBN: 978-1-4772-4949-9 (e)*

*Library of Congress Control Number: 2012913139*

# CONTENTS

# PREFACE

This powerful and convincing book, written for beginners and advanced players alike, is the only one you will need to win at craps.

The primary purpose of this book is to teach you to play craps using my tested and proven tracking numbers method. After you have acquired this knowledge, you will gain confidence in yourself and will be able to win most of the time.

The first part of this book focuses on my method. I intend to save you valuable time by not having you go through the whole book before you start playing this game. At the same time, I will provide you with sufficient and important information so that you learn to play craps the correct way in a very short time. The second part of this book gives you everything else you will need to play craps. Advanced players may not need everything in the second part, but it couldn't hurt to refresh your knowledge.

Be kind to yourself and allow yourself adequate time to read the subject matter in great detail. Study each graph to see what it means and how it will apply to you and so on, before you attempt to conquer this game. You're playing with your hard-earned dollars, and you should control this money as wisely as you can. The following pages present some of my keys and field-tested tables and graphs—follow my advice carefully. Master all of these materials, start playing this complex game, and win some money from the casinos.

# Why you want to buy my book?

This book is based on facts and figures and not as a fancy tale. I have been able to gather the actual playing craps games data, keeping track of all players in a table as to the exact point numbers come out each time, various casinos, at different locations, during all types of conditions, during a 3-5 year period. From these data, I will able to put them into different format—into some powerful tables and graphs so that you can review them and take action. I do not believe that there is another book in the market place to give you this kinds of detail and full proof methods to tackle this craps game, the correct way. Other authors may tell you that they are expert in this game, but they lack of full proof to demonstrate such event did occur and to proof their points of view.

In this book, you will see for yourself that the tables and graphs which I have provided herein are factual and that you will take notice and accept them as my proof to you that they are not just probability tables and graphs. After you have accepted my data, I will guide you through step by step as how to use them and how to play this game, the correct way and win. Once you master my methods and learn how to read my graphs, you will become an expert in this game. You will need no other book to guide you through. And this is the only book you will ever need to learn this game, the correct way. In addition, I will show you when to play heavy betting in this game and when to exist from a hot hand table game. Finally, if your follow my directions exactly as I have stated in my book, you will win some hard earned dollars from a casino anytime. And then you will tell your friends that they should buy my books for a try. So please try my book to see if you agree. Good luck.

# Disclaimer

This book is a reference guide and is not intended as the only tool you should use to make lots of money. Craps is a complex and challenging game, and it takes some time to learn it well. Craps requires lots of attention, patience, and practice. When you play, you should always plan for the worst case: losing some money. Do not expect to win every time. If you plan for potential loss, then you will cover all the bad things that could happen when you actually play. On the other hand, if everything goes well, you will profit from reading this book.

If you follow my directions and use the form I have developed to track all the events and numbers, then you will reduce the risk of losing heavily at the craps table. There is no such thing as a perfect world, so do not expect that every player is a good shooter. Expect to win a little and be happy and walk away. If you expect to win big in craps every time, then I advise you to think twice before playing this game. It is a game of chance, and there is no such thing as a sure thing. When you roll those dice, you are sometimes at slightly better odd than the dealers. Follow my guide and devise your own method to implement additional procedures and win.

This book is intended as a guide only, and there is a very high possibility of making some money if you use it correctly. If you are an aggressive player and always play heavy, watch out for your playing style—you must change your gambling strategy or your bad habit.

For example, in a good and hot table, you should play heavy for a while and then slow down to see which way the tide goes. As you win some money, be prepared to exit the table game as soon as you see sight a change. There is an old saying: you must hit heavy when it is hot, and be prepared to run away when it is cold.

I do not claim to be an expert in this game; I am merely providing you with accurate and reasonable data for you to judge and take action at your own discretion. Do not use this book as the sole tool to make your killing. Study the data and materials in this book to see if they make sense to you. Try out some small investments and test the game plan for awhile to see whether this new plan works for you. If it does not work, you should avoid using this strategy and modify your plan for a successful game.

This book is intended for beginners with little practical experience, as well as for mature craps players who have several years of practice and use their own strategy and methods. If you try my method and it does not work well, then change back to your own method. But if you practice my rules and follow them closely, you should benefit from them. Please take time to study the materials carefully before you go out and make your play.

# Overview and Introduction

The information you are about to read is factual and is based on my practice and field research over the course of three years at various casinos in the Reno and Las Vegas areas. I have recorded over 212 different players or craps shooters at different time frames throughout the day and the month. I have been able to assemble this raw data into different graphic and table formats so that you can see how to use the data to play the correct way. These tables are located throughout the book.

In this book you will also find information on craps history, the basics of the game, the way casinos operate, how to control your dice rolls, and alternative methods for playing and winning.

You should and must review each graph or table very carefully before you play this game. Otherwise, you may lose your hard-earned dollars, instead of making a nice profit by learning my methods. Please read the important sections before attempting to play this complex game. You could learn it very fast if you learn it well by following my specific instructions. It is true that you must play to win, but you must do it slowly at first and learn the process before playing heavy in this complex game.

My purpose in this book is to present my key winning strategies in the fewest words possible and then prepare you for putting it into practice by teaching my methods in the shortest possible time. I know some of you are experienced players and would prefer to use your own old methods; you may also claim that you do not have time to read the whole book. But I suggest that you at least read through my materials to see how they might benefit you before you go back to your old methods. If you read my new methods and use them correctly, you will greatly improve your chance of winning.

Gamble only with your spare money and avoid impulsive gambling. You must learn when and how to exit from a hot or cold table. This is especially true when you are winning in a very hot table, and you refuse to leave the table when you see or know that a cold hand is coming or is already there. If you remain, you could lose all of your winnings plus some of your original money.

I have over thirty years of craps experience. In the early 1980s, I was playing craps game in Reno, Nevada. I used to play at Harrah's Reno, my favorite place. I played over seven hours of craps a day for a two- to three-day trip. I usually won over a hundred dollars a day because I used two hundred as my initial investment, or capital. I usually played in the afternoon hours, from 1:00–5:30 PM. After that I took a dinner break, and then I played for another three to four hours. That was my routine schedule in Reno. At this time, I did not really know what was going on and did not know how to throw the dice.

Then my wife and I were lucky to take a three-day trip to Las Vegas. We stayed in Downtown Las Vegas at a place called Lady Luck Casino. We often played at the Horseshoe Casino, which was downtown and just a few short blocks from our hotel. I stayed at the craps table all day just to learn the game; I also learned how to throw the dice in a proper way. At the game table, I would bet twenty-five cents per game and stayed at that range for whole day. I used to change no more than a fifty-dollar bill and played with that all day. I did not really win or lose any money, breaking even most of the time.

After a five-year period of playing at the Horseshoe Casino of Las Vegas, I began gambling at the Flamingo Casino and Resort, the Paris Casino and Resort, and the Planet Hollywood Casino, all located on Las Vegas Boulevard. I spent only few hours at each casino and then sometimes moved on to the MGM Grand and spent the rest of the day there. On average, I was doing just fine because I was not losing any money, although I was still not wining money, either. This period was solely for practicing the throwing of dice and throwing them correctly.

From 1980 to 2000, I was not concerned with tracking the numbers coming out from all the shooters or players at a given table. The purpose at the time was to play and win some money. I learned how to throw the dice well so that I could make more money at times. Later, I acquired certain techniques by holding the dice in certain ways before throwing them. Most of the time, I was able to throw at least two passes or two-point numbers.

Oftentimes I threw long rolls of dices with lots of numbers coming out before I made my sevens. I was not aware that there was a method in which I could record all the numbers and place them in a proper order or to arrange them in a sequence to see what pattern these throws had in common. However, later in 2000, I was concerned about how many times I threw the dice before getting a seven to come out. I calculated that time, and it takes an average of six throws for a seven to come out. Later, I found out that was the random number prediction, and I was correct. My old data did show that number, and I was happy.

In 2005 I began thinking that there must be a way to keep record of all the number throws by all the players at that table, for one complete cycle of throwing the dice. I first started using a simple form to keep accurate records of all throws in a table. The first form has been revised several times, and the field-tested, final version is what forms the basis of my research for this book.

I have accumulated the data throughout a five-year period. In most instances, the data were derived from a craps table with at least seven players. These players were of different ages. Some of the shooters were definitely using a controlled-dice setting method, and others used random number throwing. These were typical tables and had typical throwing patterns. In some cases, I was too busy keeping track of all the throws that I did not have the opportunity to place my bets or place the correct odds for each bet.

The data I used came from the following casinos: Horseshoe Casino, Golden Nugget, the Main Station, the MGM Grand, PH Casino and Resort, Paris Casino, Bally Casino, Flamingo Casino, Harrah's Casino, Imperial Palace Casino, New York and New York, Monte Carlo, and the Excalibur Casino. My research took place at different times of day and night, and during different seasons throughout the year.

During this period of testing, I did not play with heavy hands because I am a cautious player and wanted to make sure every method I had invented was working correctly. For these reasons, I have not won very much money, but I have won consistently. And you will do the same.

I do not want to go into detail about each graph at this time, but I do want to explain what the data represents. I have used several tables or graphs to make certain points. I made the reading materials as simple as possible—you do not need to review your college algebra to see what I'm trying to do in each table. They are simple to understand and use.

To begin with, I record all throws, from shooter one to shooter ten (or as many shooters as the table can hold at that time for my recording purposes). After each throw, I record the actual throw for that first number. This process continues until I have recorded all the numbers for all the shooters for that table.

Now I have completed the recording of all the counts for that table. In between the point numbers, I record how many point numbers were made by shooter number one, how many point numbers were made by shooter number two, and so on until I have recorded the data for all shooters, for one go around. I do the same on the second around.

For example, say shooter number one made two point numbers, shooter number two did not make a point number, and neither did shooter number three. This recording would go on until I had gathered enough data on that table or left the table.

The end results of this research are quite interesting. I have found that there is a certain pattern for each number to come out, and in a certain way, as predicted by the mathematical probability outcome theory. After I developed these new methods by tracking all point numbers, hot hand or cold hand tables, solid chain table, and when to play Pass line or No Pass line, my winning hands greatly improved.

After you have a chance to read my book in detail, you should not play heavy at the beginning. Instead you should play small hands at the beginning and then gradually increase your bet as you gain practical experience and build up your confidence by using my methods. Remember, you do not have to play every hand while you are at the table. You can be an observer by watching other people play and see whether or not the table is hot or cold or a break-even table. Once you have determined the pattern in the table, you can play this game in two ways: the normal way or the opposite way, so called "Don't Pass/Don't Come" bets, with lays.

I cannot guarantee that you win every time when you play this game, even with my proven methods. However, if you follow my instructions and employ my methods correctly, you would be a much better player than if you had not used my methods at all. Your chance of winning will increase—I have field tested each method, and they work well. Currently there are no better tools in the market than the ones I have perfected in this book. Once you have mastered all of my methods, you will feel secure and confident and be ready to do some actual gambling—and to win some money. But remember to play with caution, patience, and tolerance. Play with small sums at a time, and then gradually increase your bets as you gain practical experience.

# PART I:
# THE TRACKING NUMBERS METHOD

# CHAPTER 1:
# STRATEGY AND PLANNING

Your ultimate plan is to play until you win some money. Do not plan to win big at any given time. "Be happy and be merry" is your main motto. Play only if you use my system, keeping track all the point numbers and recording them correctly, and know exact numbers for when each number appears and how many of those numbers have not yet appeared. Keep accurate accounting record because that's your blood and butter. Make sure to concentrate on those point numbers not yet come out; they will come out later. You will be rewarded later on if you take my method into account.

In this chapter you will learn how to design your game plan. When you arrive at a craps table for the very first time, you may ask yourself the following questions: Do I want to play the normal way, or do I want to play the opposite game (Don't Come or Don't Pass)? Do I just play the field bets? Do I play the horn bets? Do I play all the hard numbers bets? Do I play the pass line, the place bets, or a combination of any other bets together?

Whichever you choose, you are planning and that is good. I suggest that you observe the first few throws to see whether or not the shooter can make a point number. After that, you can make your next move. There are many correct methods to choose from, but each method has a limitation. This is the only casino game in the world that you can play both good or bad hands at the same time. Once you have decided which way is best for you, you must learn how to concentrate, how to bet, and when to bet heavy and employ my methods correctly.

There are six point numbers: 4, 5, 6, 8, 9, and 10. They are located just in front of each dealer on both ends of the table. When the first or a new shooter comes in, he must throw a point number (7 or 11) the very first time. If the shooter throws a point number, then he must try to make that point number—roll his point number again—before he throws a 7. If he throws a 7, he loses, and almost every bet on the table loses, too.

You can bet on these point numbers at any time, but the proper way, in a good or normal condition table, is to bet on the pass line the very first time. When a shooter throws a point number and you play a pass line, you should always play with the maximum casino-allowed odds. This odd is in your favor because the casino will pay you with extra money or bonus when you win. This is the only added advantage you will get when you first play with the pass line. For example, when a point number 5 or 9 is established, you can place the maximum allowed odds just behind the pass line bet.

In Harrah's Casino and Hotel at Las Vegas, the maximum odd is four times of your pass line amount. If you are betting just $5 in the pass line, and the point number is 5, for example, you can place a $20 chip behind the pass line. If the shooter throws a 5 on the next throw, you win. Your return would be as follows: $5 for the pass line amount, and $30 for the odds you place, for a total of $35. From this play, you would gain an extra $10 because you play with maximum odds. This is your only casino advantage, by taking advantage of casino-allowed odds, because a $2 odd will get back $3. You must also place maximum allowed odds when you play the come out bet, when the point number is established.

Even when you play the pass line bet or the come out bet, the casino still has a 5 percent advantage over your bets. If you decide to play any other way besides these two methods, your chance of winning is much less. You may only have a 45 percent chance of winning by employing different ways than what I have mentioned here. No matter what your bets are the first time or second time, the house has an added advantage over you. Play smart and employ my methods at all times. Perhaps you should consider playing both 6 and 8 at all times, two bets at a time, and you can outperform a 7 because you have a ten-to-six advantage. But, in this situation, you will lose more if the 7 comes before your two point numbers.

When you win some money, you should at least take back all of your initial investments before you continue to play. After the full return of all your capital, you can afford to gamble the profit you have made thus far. After a winning hand, you should ask the dealers to "Take down all my bets." At that time, your total bets will be returned or given back to you. You could continue to play the same game or wait for the next hand. Avoid playing the field bets even if you see there are seven large numbers on that field, which you think would give you a winning hand. In fact, if you play the field bets, the house has a 20 percent advantage over you.

After researching all your options, your best bets are limited to the following: pass line or come out line, with maximum allowed odds in the back. Next in line are the place bets and then the no pass or no come bets, with maximum lays on each. Avoid all other bets if possible. In chapter 5, you can see how you stand against the house in various situations. Do not gamble with risky bets—make every bet count. You are here to win some spare money and walk away quickly once you have won a small profit. Do not stay very long at any table.

Another area of consideration is to determine how much capital you need to start the game, and how much capital you can afford to lose without any hardship to your pocket book. You must play with spare money sitting in your drawer at home and earning no interest, money you are ready to give away without any difficulty. Please remember, do not gamble on your monthly payroll check or your normal living expenses. Also, you must maintain a large sum of liquid cash on hand at all times to take care of emergency use. You must think in terms of losing this money and giving it to the house, and you still have enough money left over for your next game, and for your food and drinks, and to go back home? This planning is very crucial because for certain reasons, if you did lose this money, you will still be able to play the same game for the duration of the trip. Some people are not so lucky because they spend more than they can afford and end up with little or no money left for the remainder of the trip. You do not want to copy their bad planning and habits. You are different and plan wisely.

You should also set up your short-term and long-term gambling goals. Stay away from an impulsive gambling attitude. Control your emotions and keep calm at all times; don't blame on yourself if you lose some money because it happens to everyone.

# When to Play

Playing craps requires careful planning. Many craps players are not paying special attention when they play this game. They think that this is a simple and easy money-making game, so they do not care how and where they throw the dice. They just walk in any craps table, start with just $20, and immediately place their bets in a proper box without knowing what has taken place before they arrive. This is a common error, and you do not want to do that. You play with caution and patience because you are different, and you want to spend your hard-earned dollars in a prudent way.

When you play this game, you play with patience, caution, and tolerance. You play only with your bonus money, your spare money. Do not play with your mortgage payment, utilities money, or retirement account. Your goal is to win some and walk away as quick as you can. Do not wait for the other players if they still remain after a very hot hand table. Walk away, take a break, and drink some water, or go to see a movie and come back much later. Do not go back to the same old table again; go to some other table and observe before playing there.

Be careful in selecting the right table before you play. Do not just go to any table and start playing. You should pay attention to all kinds of conditions. For example, you should avoid a table with lots of distractions, where people are drinking and talking aloud and do not pay attention to what they are doing. Also, avoid a table where more people are leaving than coming. Do not go to a table where people complain that it is the coldest table in the world. Look for positives: Do the players have long strings of chips in front of them? Do they look happy? Are they all shouting for the shooter to make a certain number? If this is the case, you should play at that table if you can.

As you learn to keep tabs on the number of shooters who made point numbers versus the number of shooters who made no point numbers, you will get some ideas as how good a table you have and where to go from here. If you have more good shooters (those who make point numbers) than bad shooters (those who made no point numbers), then you have a reasonably good table. Under this condition, you can afford to play heavy and plan to exit the game as soon as the tide is turning. For example, if you witness three or four consecutive shooters who can make point numbers consistently, then it is okay to play heavy. The opposite is also true: when you encounter a table in which four different shooters have not made a point number, the fifth shooter will likely not make a point number. In this situation you should wait or play the don't pass line instead.

If you keep a full accounting of point numbers, you will have a much better opportunity to win than playing randomly. Also, if you pay attention and track your numbers correctly, you will gain a great deal of confidence in playing this game. Perhaps you my even play heavy on those numbers not yet come out. For instance, point number 6 has been thrown thirty times, and yet point number 8 came out just fifteen times. You would confidently say, "I would have a much better chance of winning if I were to bet on 8 than number 6 due to the number of times each number has thrown or been already recorded."

You may also say that these two numbers are similar in nature and also act as a pair, because both have the same number of ways for the dice to come out with that number. This is so because these two numbers tend to come very close, in the number of throws, if you were to keep tabs of these numbers over a prolonged period of time. Eventually these two point numbers cancel each other—that is, no one number is greater than the others. It is also true to the other pairs of numbers—say, 4 or 10, 5 or 9—because they also act as companions, and the outcome for each pair is the same.

Remember through all of this that the good hands must also equal the bad hands. The number of shooters who make point number is almost equivalent to the number of shooters who do not make point number. For instance, a good shooter shoots three point numbers, and then come three bad shooters who make no point number. This is called the dead even throw. I have seldom witnessed this event during two or three hours of continuous playing. However, I *have* seen that there are slightly more shooters who make point numbers than shooters who do not make any point numbers. So watch out for these kinds of activities. You can win under this condition.

It is believed by using a mathematical model, this so-called *x* number of good throws must equal the total number of bad throws over a three-hour period using a random throwing method. But if you play in a table in which shooters are setting their dice and controlling the force of their throws, then you will gain a slight edge over the house. A controlled throwing method normally tends to give the shooter a better winning chance than one using a randomly throwing method. In chapter 13 you will learn to recognize dice control methods.

When you go to a table, watch for a while to see if you can spot some veteran shooters. This table should be yours. Pay full attention to what you are doing at that table, and you should maintain a happy attitude. You should first play with a small amount and see which way the tide is turning. After a few plays or a few shooter shooters, you should have a reasonably good idea of what to expect this table to do for you. Remember, you must keep track of the first four hands in any given table to see whether or not you should stay in that table. To stay, you must have won two of the four hands; otherwise, you should be playing at another table. If you find that there is a pattern, such as the first three shooters can make several pass points or point numbers, then you have a decent table and should pay full attention and play well. On the other hand, if you find that not a single shooter can make one point number, you'd better play don't pass or don't come, or you can just walk away and save your money.

# Different Ways to Play

Craps is quite complex, yet it has many advantages over other table games and slot machine games. For example, by placing on the pass line or come line with maximum odds, and the don't pass or don't come line bets, also with maximum lays, the house only has a very slight edge over you, 0.15 percent, which is almost dead even. Craps bets are the highest return on your investment than any other casino table game.

There are many ways to begin playing the game; certain ways will yield more, and others will yield less in return. You must place your bet before the shooter starts to throw the dices or the stickman will declare there are no bets. When the shooter throws either a 7 or 11, and you place your money in the pass line, you win. This is also called the two ways win. But you also have a three ways chance to lose if the shooter throws a 2, 3, or 12. If the shooter throws a point number, such as 4, 5, 6, 8, 9,or 10, and then the shooter rolls a 7 on the next throw before a point number, it is called a seven out, and you lose. This includes all the bets on that table, no matter what. The come out roll is the same as the first throw, and the shooter must make a point number or a no number. If she makes a point number in a come out roll, then the dealer will place the on-off sticker on that number, which is called the point box number. This on-off box is also called the puck. The point box number stays on the table until the shooter either throws the point number again or makes a seven out. Then the punk will return to the dealer, and the off position will show on top. This means that the table will now begin a new game, and you must place your bets before the player shoots a number or begins to throw the dice.

In your first hand or at the beginning of a new shooter, you can bet on the pass line or don't pass line, horn bets (2, 3, 11, and 12), field bets (2, 3, 4, 9, 10, 11, 12), hard numbers (4, 6, 8, 10), big red, big 6 or 8, any 7s, don't pass line, the world bet, and a place bet. If 7 is the first roll number, other than a horn number (2, 3, 11, and 12), you will lose on the following bets: don't pass, horn bets, field bets, hard numbers, big 6 or 8, and place bet, if they are working. The people who have the following numbers will win for that roll: pass line, big red, and world bet. If you put just $5 in the pass line, that is what you will get back. The $5 bet for the big red would get $20, and the world bet would break even. But if that shooter makes no 7 on the first roll or throws a horn numbers, then he would make a point number, such as 4, 5, 6, 8, 9, or 10.

For our purpose, let's say that shooter throws a 6 as a come out point number; then the shooter must make that point number before a 7 comes. Let us assume that you have a pass line bet of $10, and then you place a maximum-allowed odds, say 5 × $10 = $50, as your odds, a total investment of $60. And let us assume that the shooter does throw a 6 before a 7, after few throws. Then you would be rewarded in the amount of the $10 return for your pass line bet, plus $60 for your odd bets, for a total of $70, because the $5 odds will give you $6 in return, or 20 percent profit, This is also your advantage over the house.

If you have $50 odds, this will give you a return of $60. A $60 investment would turn that into $70 for you, a $10 profit, which is 16.6 percent return. You get the same return for the number 8 because 6 and 8 are identical in nature or so-called pair numbers, and will yield the same in return. Therefore it is true for numbers 4 and 10, and 5 and 9, because they are the similar pairs, and we sometimes call them brother and sister; that is the reason for the yield of having the same return for both pair numbers.

If the shooter throws a number, other than horn numbers or 7, then he makes a point number on the first throw; that number is called the point number. If he throws a 7 before the point number, then we call that a seven out, and everyone loses other than the player who bet on the don't pass line.

After the shooter throws a point number, you can do many things. The most favorable bet is on the come out line on the second throw. One benefit to betting on the come out line on the second throw is that most shooters do throw another similar number later on in the game, and then you will fully recapture your investment. But you can bet on a place line, horn bets, hard numbers, big red, world bet, field numbers, three-way hop bets, and so on. All these bets, except the come line bet, are not so favorable to you because the odds against you are greater than before due to the numbers of times the shooter has already thrown. If you continue to place your bet, you will lose more than you would gain from it. The come line bet is similar to the pass line bet, and if you place maximum odds on the come line bet, you will be much better off due to your odds on that come out bet number (the point number for your come bet). The house gives you this advantage. It is possible that you would get a 10 percent advantage over the house by doing it this way, but if you do not put any odds on a come out bet point number, then you will not come out ahead, and you will be losing because the house has a 2 percent point advantage over you. When you play the pass line or come out line bets, please put maximum odds on these plays.

A place bet is a little different than the pass line bet. It has certain advantage because you can place these bets anytime before a seven will come up. Normally, you would place money in any of six numbers—4, 5, 6, 8, 9, and 10—at any time, even before the start of the new shooter. In most instances, these numbers are not working due to the first time throwing a 7 at the beginning of a new game. That is the reason for you to announce that your numbers are not working on the first throw of the dice. But you must tell the dealer that these numbers are off for the first throw; they are working only when you have a point number established. When the shooter throws one of your place numbers on the second throw, for example, then you win money for that number. Let us say that the shooter throws 4 as a number, and you place $10 on number 4. You would return a sum of $18. Under normal conditions, you would buy $25 on a 4 or a 10, and if that number comes out on the next throw, your net return would be $49, because you must pay the dealer $1 as commission.

You can bet on horn bets anytime. Normally you would do better at the beginning of a new shooter. You can place $5 on the horn bet. If the throw is a 12, then you would get back $32.75, if you have a calculator. Otherwise, the house would just give you back $30. You could dispute this difference if you have the time and the calculator on hand for your dispute. Otherwise, they think they are right and pay you off quickly to avoid any further complication. But the players and dealers are not happy with you if you delay the game any longer.

You can place in your bet in the hard numbers, such as 4, 6, 8, or 10. The return for your hard 6 or 8 on a $5 bet is 10:1, and the return for your 4 or 10 is 8:1. So your chance of getting these numbers is very remote. The house has a huge advantage over you on these numbers. The dealers would normally ask if anyone who wants a hard number, and he will continue to announce that until someone takes a bite. Remember, hitting a hard 6 or 8 or any other hard number, 4 or 10, is only a 11 percent chance, but if you hit one of them, your reward is great. That is the reason for the stickman to announce such a big deal at the beginning of the throw, to catch some small fish.

Playing the field numbers is very simple. Most beginners are attracted to this area because there are so many numbers in the field, such as 2, 3, 4, 9, 10, 11, and 12. They think that they have an advantage over the house; they see these numbers and do not realize that these are one-time throws. They are deadly wrong because the house has a 6 percent advantage over them on these numbers. You have a much better chance of getting a 7 than these numbers, so play this game diligently and try to avoid this as much as you can. Some say that these are suckers bets. Remember, these are one-time bets, one throw only, so do not expect a huge return. Your best bet is the place bet because you can take back your bet at any time. With the pass line or come out line, the bets you place are non-returnable, except your place odds.

There are other ways to play, and some casinos offer different configurations and formats. Few casinos offer ten-number bets, such as 2, 3, 4, 5, 6, 8, 9, 10, 11, and 12. This game is often called the craps-less game because the first throw is the point number, for practical purposes. The shooter must make this same number in order to win the game and odds. But you still can place your bets in other slots or boxes, you will win when that number is thrown. If the first throw is a 6, for example, and your pass line bet is $5, then you're at $25 for your odds. For you to win, the shooter must hit the 6 before throwing a 7. The return is the same as before; depending on the odds, $6 is your return. If on the next new game, the shooter throws a

11, for example, and you have a $5 bet, now you place another $5 for your odds. If an 11 is thrown, in a later throw you will win on the 11 the $5 you first placed, plus the $5 odd × 15, for $75 total. Other numbers would do similar things and similar returns. But you must make that point number before 7 comes out.

Playing craps game is exciting and rewarding if you play it right. You have many ways to place your bet, and the outcome and payoff for each is very different. The normal way is to place a bet at the pass line at the very beginning of the game. For practical purposes, however, it is best to place odds behind your first point number, the maximum odds allowed by the casino. You make more money on the odds you place behind your pass line bet. Then the next move is to place a bet to the come line. When that number is established, it is your second point number. Then you should place maximum odds behind that point number. You may consider betting the come bet for the second time. If you do, then you have three different point numbers to work for you. Later, when your number is called, this is your first return bet. Later still, when your second number is announced, this is your second return for your come out bet. Now you only have one number working for you: the pass line bet number. If you make that number, then you have a return of all three numbers, which is very good.

Now that you have recouped all of your investment in the pass line, plus the profit of the odds you placed behind the point number plus a full return on the two come out bets, what are you going to do next? This depends on the kind of table—hot or cold, long roll of throwing of dices or not. If the next beginning throw is a 7, then you may think in turns of trying the same method, except this time place only on the come out bets, or just put the money on the place bets. You can wait to see how well the same shooter is performing in turns of throwing numbers. Can he continue making or throwing numbers? How many of these numbers can he throw without hitting a 7? You may need to evaluate this condition for a while just to see where you stand in relationship to the overall performance of the game. If the shooter continues making numbers after a long roll of throwing, you must play heavy and pay attention to the shooter to see which direction the game will go. Such a good table is difficult to find, so pay attention and play cautiously—and get ready to run when the tide is turning. When you win some profit, be ready to move on and retire for awhile. Do not continue playing without taking some kind of break. You could lose all of the money you gain if you do not plan for an exit strategy.

From time to time, you must keep track of the point numbers made by each shooter and record them in the proper format using the tables I have provided in this book. With this method, you will know whether or not the shooter or shooters will bring you profit if you continue playing at the table. At the same time, check to see how much money you have won or lost so far, and then plan which method is better for you, good hand method or bad hand method. It is up to you to select the proper way to play this game and still win.

## Playing Don't Bets

There are other ways to play this game, and these should be incorporated into your strategy. The opposite way, which is the don't pass or don't come line bets, is popular and proper. I have seen players make lots of money by employing such a method. But these players, whom I watched at the Silver Legacy in 2009, did not take advantage of the big winning hands, and they did not plan for an exit strategy. At the end, they lost money instead winning. I first noticed them while I was playing the place line bets. These two high rollers bet $25 at the beginning on Don't Pass line. When a point number was established, they placed the maximum lays for that particular point number. They won that game again and again, maybe six times. Yet they still played with the same style and method without an Exist plan. I noticed that they could easily won over a thousand dollars, just by playing the don't pass lines, but they were too eager to win more. In the end, they lost all of the gains plus some of their investments. But you will not do that by using my method, because you have already have an exit plan to take care of that misfortunate.

Sometimes when you play the don't pass line, people will give you a dirty look, but do not let this hinder you. If you see the table is turning cold, go ahead and play with the don't pass or don't come bets. Let the other players continue playing their old style and lose. You are different because you have several methods to play this game. You do not care whether the table is hot or cold. You play the game in accordance with the current conditions. If the table is hot, you play the pass line and come out bet, with maximum odds. If the table is cold, you do not have to continue playing the same style like everyone else. You can be different, and that is the main reason that craps is so different from any other table game.

About five years ago, I witnessed the worst table in my life. I saw a table consisting of ten different shooters who made no point numbers. That was a very long time, and it was very unusual table, the longest no point number table I had seen for over three years. . If you were playing in this table with the don't pass line bets, you could have made a fortunate if you also played heavy. But of course, no one could predict this event, so not too many people could made much money at this table. I was lucky to play don't pass lines, but my bets were very marginal, although I did make some profit.

If you are playing a very bad table, try the don't pass line with maximum lays. Play in such a table only if you see first three shooters, where one shooter throw three times and hits a 7, and the second shooter throws three times and hits a 7, and the third shooter throws just two times before hitting a 7. You can bet heavy on the fourth shooter. Do not place any more don't pass line bets if you see two consecutive shooters who make point numbers. After that, you must change your playing method to a good hand method, or you risk losing it all.

For better or worse, there are a variety of ways to make your bets. You must practice with patience to see which method is better for you. Do you want to concentrate on just the pass line and come out lines, or do you care to take other options, such as don't pass or don't come out bets? I would prefer to do both in the event certain conditions call for me to change my gambling plans, and you should do the same. That is no shame to everyone if you play don't pass line instead of the normal bet of placing money in the pass line for the beginning throw.

If you see a bad hand, please switch your plan. You have no direct connection to your next player; he does not pay for your mortgage or buying your food. You do not care what others are doing as long as you can employ good strategy over them. You are better than them in turns of playing this game in a correct manner.

Do not just play and expect to win. You must have some game plans. If you do not have adequate planning, the house will certainly take advantage of you. Also, you will not win as much as you would like if you stick with just one method of playing this exciting game. The table conditions will dictate the best way for you to play, so plan wisely, adapt to the current conditions, and employ several tools whenever you put your money down at a table.

# CHAPTER 2:
# THE FIVE MAIN METHODS

You are now ready to play some craps the correct way. I will briefly explain my five proven methods, one at a time, but you must promise me that you will also continue to read the rest of the book. By doing so, you will have a better understanding of all my methods, and you will do well in your games. There are a number of different tables or graphs in this book. For this chapter I have specifically selected only four of these tables, and I've provided you with enough information so that you once you have learned these methods, you are ready to play this game.

Of these four tables, one of the most important forms you will ever need is Table A, "Tracking All Point Numbers and No Point Numbers." You should get familiar with this form and carry it with you when you play. Don't go out and play craps without taking this important form with you. It will keep track of all activities at a given table, no matter what kinds of numbers come out or what kinds of shooters throw the dice.

At first you may feel that this form is too large to carry along with you when you play, that it might attract unintended attention. The casino boss, or boxman might ask you what you are doing with that form you carry, other players may question you, and so on. Do not be discouraged or ashamed. Just play your game.

When I play this craps game in Las Vegas, people look at me to see what I'm doing with my form and ask why I'm using it. My reply is that I am doing a school research project, and this is my way of keeping track of the table game. I do not give them any more information. I do not let them know how the table is performing, nor do I give them any advice about how to play the game.

There is no law to prohibit you from using your form to record the activities in that table if you are playing their game. You do not need to show them what you have and how your system works, but you must not write on the rail with ink. Otherwise you will be notified with unkind words from the boxman or pit bull at the back of the table. Also, play with polite manners and do not cause problems with the casino people. Talk to your neighbors and keep up a happy and cheerful demeanor while recording your throw counts and point number counts.

If you feel that you have been intimidated by the players next to you, or by the dealers or by someone else in the table, I have a solution for you. Your embarrassment is easily overcome. I have been intimidated on many occasions. Usually I simply ignore them, but I have devised a method using $1 casino chips as my counting devices. When I arrive at a new table for the first time, I ask for change of $400. I also ask the dealer to change a $20 into $1 chips. I will use these $1 chips as my counting and recording device.

The best place to hide yourself is at the end of the table, next to either side of the dealers. You will have plenty of rack space to keep track of all point numbers thrown or no point number thrown. When I play at the end of the table, I have plenty room to keep track of all players in a table. I use the top rack for good hand (G) and using the lower rack for bad hand (B). I place my chips in the exact manner that I show on Table A, in the proper columns and rolls. When you see one player leave and then later a new player comes to take his place, this is okay. You will track this new player the same way as the old player. There is no difference either way. Suppose that the dice have already passed on to other players in the table, far from the new player or next to the new player who just came in. The outcome is the same. The thrower of the dice at any given time makes no difference to the outcome of future events.

## Table A: Tracking All Point Numbers and No Point Numbers (Using $1 Chips)

| Column | 1 | 2 | 3 | 4 | 5 | 6 | 7 | 8 | 9 | 10 |
|---|---|---|---|---|---|---|---|---|---|---|
| Good Point Numbers Made by a Shooter | 0 | 0 0 |  | 0 0 | 0 | 0 | 0 |  |  |  |
| Bad Number of Shooters made No Point Number | 0 0 |  | 0 0 0 |  | 0 | 0 | 0 |  |  |  |

*Note: Under row G (good), we have a total of six shooters who made eight point numbers. Under row B (bad), we have eight shooters who made no point numbers. For example, in column 1, I used one $1 chip to represent the first shooter, who made a point number. Then in the second row, which is the B row and represents the no point shooters, I use two chips to represent two shooters, who did not make a point number. Under this condition, I call this even-steven, no win and no lose.*

As you can see in Table A, I use two rows in one column: one roll for good hands (G) and another roll for bad hands (B). I always use a new shooter as my beginning point. I do not use a shooter who has already thrown many times or has already made one or more point numbers. I start from a new shooter. When a new shooter throws one point number, I will use a $1 chip to record this point number under column 1, roll 1. This is the only point number made by that shooter. I call this shooter number one. The dice are passed on to the next shooter, shooter two, who does not make a point number. The dice are passed on to shooter three, and he does not make a point number, either. I place two $1 chips in column one, but on the lower row, which we use letter (B) for no point shooters, or bad hands. After that, we start with shooter four, who throws two point numbers. I will use two $1 chips to represent the point numbers made by shooter four in column two, tow one, which we call the good hand (G). Then we have shooters five, six, and seven, and all of them make no point numbers. We record this, using chips, in column three, but in row B, by using three $1 chips to represent these no point number shooters.

In Table A, we have recorded the table activities for fourteen shooters. Some of them might have thrown more than once as the dice pass from person to person around the table. A typical table may allow only ten people. At this table, from time to time you should review the total point numbers in the top row, as compared to the total no point numbers in the lower row. Then you can get a better idea about the overall performance of the table at any given time. For Table A, we have six shooters who have thrown eight point numbers, and we have eight shooters who did not make a point number. This is an even game, eight point numbers and eight no point numbers. What should you do under this condition? You should walk way and stop playing this game, saving you some money for later use. On the other hand, if you see there are more point numbers made than no point numbers made, you should stay and play this game until the changing hands occur.

Another method I often use is shown on Table B, "Record the Number of Throws." This method is important because you are recording all the points numbers thrown in a given table with all the different players in a given table. Some of the shooters may have thrown more than once in this go around. This method is used to track all six point numbers to see which of these are underperformed and which are overperformed. This method is good to use in any casino game environment.

| | 1 | 2 | 3 | 4 | G | 0 0 | 0 | 0 | (3 shooters made 4 point numbers) |
|---|---|---|---|---|---|---|---|---|---|
| | 1 | 2 | 3 | 4 | . | 00 0 | 0 | | (4 shooters made no point numbers) |
| | | | | | | | | | |
| | | | | | | | | | |
| | | | | | | | | | |
| True % | | | | | | Actual % thrown | | | |
| | | 1 2 3 4 5 6 7 | | | | | | | |
| | 4 | | | | | 12 | 24% | | |
| 25 % | | 1 2 3 4 5 | | | | | | | |
| | 10 | | | | | | | | |
| | | 1 2 3 4 5 6 7 8 9 10 | | | | | | | |
| | 5 | | | | | 17 | 34% | | |
| 33 % | | 1 2 3 4 5 6 7 | | | | | | | |
| | 9 | | | | | | | | |
| | | 1 2 3 4 5 6 7 8 9 10 11 | | | | | | | |
| | 6 | | | | | 21 | 42% | | |
| 42 % | | 1 2 3 4 5 6 7 8 9 10 | | | | | | | |
| | 8 | | | | | | | | |
| | | | | | | | | | |
| | | | | | | | | | |

**Table B—Record the Numbers of Point Numbers Throws At a Given Time**

On Table B, you will record any of the six point numbers (4, 5, 6, 8, 9, and 10) after each throw, except horn bet numbers (2, 3, 11, 12) or 7. Do not reuse Table B when you go to a new table. You must use a new form each time you go to a new table, so you do not mix new and old data together. Each table should stand by itself. For example, for point numbers 4 or 10, when the first shooter throws a 4 the first time, you will write down a one on the row where the "4" appears. If a second thrown number is also 4, then you would write down a two in the same row. The process of recording all other point numbers is the same. After you have played this game for one or two hours, you must do a short math calculation to see how you stand in relationship to the true probability for each point

19

number. The true point numbers are shown on the far left side of the table, such as a 25 percent chance for 4 or 10 to appear in a given time frame, a 33 percent chance for a 5 or 9 to appear in a given throw, and finally a 42 percent chance for a throw of 6 or 8. From this table, you will see that you are not too far from the true calculation.

The actual throws for 4 or 10 is 24 percent, versus the 25 percent probability value. You can see the other actual thrown point numbers come very close to the true value under the probability expectation. Based on these point numbers thrown, you will notice that you will have a better advantage of placing bets for 9 and 10 because there will be more of these numbers to come out in the future throws than the other point numbers that already came out, such as 4, 5, 6, and 8. You can concentrate your bets just by watching which of these point numbers have not come out very often as compared to those point numbers already thrown. Do a brief calculation from time to time to see exactly how you stand; it does not take up very much time, and it is for your own good, if you follow my method. From this table, the play bet for 10 is my best choice.

We have so far discussed some basic accounting records for keeping track of all point numbers 4, 5, 6, 8, 9, and 10. We now shift our focus to a new area. You need to know how many people in your full table will throw one point number, how many people will throw two point numbers, and so on. It is necessary for you to pay full attention to this new area because it is the meat of my book, and I will explain the findings in the following manner. From my raw data, I have been able to calculate the percentage of shooters who will make one point number, how many shooters in the same table will make two point numbers, and so on.

From Table C, "The Game of Chances Method," you will see that only 50 percent of the shooters will shoot one point number. After that, 29.2 percent of shooters will throw two point numbers, 10.8 percent of shooters at the table will throw three point numbers, and only 0.5 percent of total shooters will throw eight point numbers or point passes. This rule is simple: The more you throw without your point number coming out first, the greater risk you will get and the chance of throwing a seven out instead of your particular point number. You can see from Table C that it is harder and harder to get more point passes or point numbers after the very first point number.

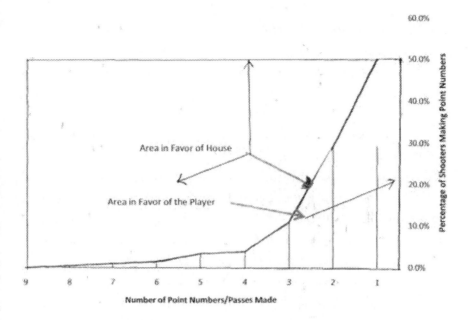

Table C Game of Chance - Shooters Making the Point Number

This method is very helpful because it gives you a tool to identify when to play heavy and when to exit the game table. It gives you the information you need to know about your chance of winning in any given time. Study this table very carefully and use it wisely, because it will save your hard-earned money if you follow my directions. If you don't follow my instructions, you could lose a lot of your dollars, and you will not be happy.

Remember, when we talk about the first point number, we mean the first number you established at the beginning, and later you must throw that number before a 7. For the second point number, you already made the first point number. Then you will begin to throw at the start of a new game, and later you will throw another point number, such as 8. After a few throws, the shooter will make or throw a point number 8 before the 7 comes out. Then you have thrown 2 point numbers. If you were to continue this game, your outcome is very remote because you have only a 20 percent chance of getting the next six numbers, these point numbers, 4, 5, 6, 7, 8, and 9, to fulfill your objective.

After you make the first three point numbers, you should play light and watchful. Pay attention to the shooter; do not listen to the surrounding players who encourage you to play heavy. You already made your profit—why do you want to give that away? Finally, down the line, your chance of getting more point numbers, after the fourth point number comes out, is only 6 percent, not very high. You should not be playing this game at that time. You should watch to see which way the table will turn and then play in accordance with the outcome at that time.

I encourage you to study this graph and get a better understanding of its implications before you go out and play. You can test this method by playing a small sum first, and later you can increase your bets to suit your taste and style. But I must caution you that you should not play don't pass lines if you see a shooter who throws a point number first, then throws two times and makes another point number; this process goes on and on for fast point number throwing. If this happens, you have a hot hand table and should play the good method, normal pass lines and come out bet lines. Otherwise, you must change hands to play the opposite game.

This table is the most important of all my tables because it shows the chance of making more than the first point number and thus the probability of winning more money after the first point number. As always, please remember that you must limit your liability and play only with what you can afford to lose.


My next method is represented in Table D, "Tracking a Hot Hand Table—Solid Chain Method." From the table D you can see that a break-even game happened at the beginning. People were moving from table to table, and though this does not affect your tracking ability, you must be very patience to start with this game. Patience is a virtue, and although waiting is hard to do, you must wait until such an opportunity comes your way. Finding such a hot hand table would require lots of time and effort and is a rare occurrence. On average, you would find such a hot hand table every two to three days, after you have spent at least three hours of continuous playing at a given table. And you must take a seven-day trip to enjoy it. If you find such a hot hand table, you find a gold mine, but this table should last only an hour or so.

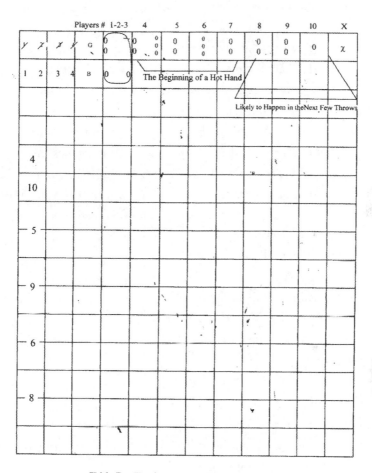

| Players # | 1-2-3 | | | 4 | 5 | 6 | 7 | 8 | 9 | 10 | X |
|---|---|---|---|---|---|---|---|---|---|---|---|
| y | x | x | x | G | 0 0 | 0 0 0 | 0 0 0 | 0 0 0 | 0 0 0 | 0 0 0 | 0 | x |
| 1 | 2 | 3 | 4 | B | 0 0 | | | | | | | |

The Beginning of a Hot Hand

Likely to Happen in theNext Few Throws

**Table D—Tracking a Hot Table-Solid Chain**

Please remember that for this table and all other tables using this form, the top line represents just one shooter and the bottom line can represent many shooters. One small circle is one shooter, and two circles represents two shooters.

From Table D, you can see that shooter one makes two point numbers, but shooters two and three could not make any point numbers. I record these two shooters under "B," the bad shooter row, with two circles. This first column takes up three different shooters, one on the top and two on the bottom. After these shooters, we will begin to see the opening of a very hot hand, also called the solid gold chain. This process starts with shooter four: see this number on the very top of the page, with the title called Player Number on the far left side.

As you can see in the above table, shooter four makes five point numbers. I use five small circles under the row with the letter "G," which stands for a good shooter. This follows by shooter five, the next column, who makes two point numbers. Then shooter six comes to play, and he too makes three point numbers. Shooter seven makes two point numbers, as well as shooters eight and nine. But shooter ten makes only 1 point number. The results are recorded and shown on Table D. Finally, shooter X, or the next player, also makes *x* point numbers, or unknown numbers at this time. We're just guessing this event could happen this way. It is 100 percent certain that shooters eight to eleven could make point numbers. After that we cannot tell which way the game will go. From Table D, you have witnessed a very impressive and outstanding table, with the beginning of a solid five point numbers thrown by shooter four, and all the way to shooter X, each makes a point number or more to create this unusual chain. You do not see this kind of solid chain table very often. If you do, please play heavy.

Under this solid chain condition, you can tell the solid foundation created by the first four point number shooters, shooters four to seven, in which each makes at least two point numbers. Then at the beginning of shooter eight, he too makes two point numbers. This is definitely the beginning of a very good hand. After shooter eight, you should play extremely heavy hands through the next four shooters. You should concentrate heavy bets on the first two point numbers, and play less on the three point number, and so on, which is based on the Table C, the probability curve table. After you have played at this solid gold chain table for awhile, then you will see the cold hand coming. You will witness two or three consecutive no point number hands. At that time, you must exit from this table without further notice. Take your money and run fast. If you do want to play some more, then you ought to consider playing the bad hand games, the don't come and don't pass lines.

The next good method is called the hit and run method. I do not have a table for this event, but it can greatly benefit your game plan. Under this condition, what you need to remember is to play heavy when you see a solid chain table and run away when you see bad shooters coming, or exit the table as soon as you have won some casino money. To witness this hit and run table, you must be patient and wait for opportunity. You should observe and pay attention to a table in which the players are yelling and laughing and calling on the shooter to throw that certain point number for everyone at the table to win. You may notice that all of the players have a long string of high-value chips in front of them, and some of them even put some of these chips in their pockets to hide them. This is a good indication of a very hot table.

You should play this table with ease and comfort if you can get in or find space for you to play. But you must not force your way in, because other players might not like you. To get into such a hot hand table, you should always carry some loose change or some large size chips, and then make changes when you enter such a table without disturbing the shooter. You do not want to interrupt the hot hand shooter in the middle of the game. You must allow this hot shooter to continue throwing good numbers, hand after hand, so that you can win some money. There should be no prolonged interruption or delay. Sometimes you will see the dealers or casino boss yell at a player to distract the shooter's attention and hope that the shooter will make a mistake and throw out the 7, so that the house can win.

# CHAPTER 3:
# THE ULTIMATE FORM FOR
# TRACKING NUMBERS

Sometimes you may need another method to keep track of your numbers. At Table 7, "The Ultimate Form for Tracking Numbers," you will see that I have included a separate column on the bottom of this form, showing the number of 7s and number of horns. These two extra boxes can assist you to further your knowledge of tracking all the different outcomes for a pair of dice. This is a better system to let us know the overall activities at the table, one number at a time, no matter which number would come out from the throw. From Table 7, you will see the box number for the number of 7s. When you witness a throw of 7, either in the beginning of the throw or when the shooter throws a 7 before a point number, you will record the times it appears in that box.

When you have enough information, you can decide what course of action you will take. For instance, a 7 will come out when you throw six times on the dices, no matter what numbers come out at any given time; please read the probability curve table for interpretation. What this means is that while you are tracking all the activities at the table, the more you throw the dices without throwing your point numbers first, the more chance of throwing the 7 than your number. You may say to yourself, "This is too complicated and I cannot win." That is not the case if you come to a hot hand table with a long throw, or a solid gold chain table, or a short hub with point number table. You still can win.

What do I mean that the 7 comes out for every six throws? When you keep track on Table 7, you will record full activities at all times. It is not necessary that every six throws there has to be a 7. Sometimes you will see a good shooter throws thirty times without hitting a 7. Then the next shooter may throw twenty times before hitting a 7. But these two good shooters are not doing you a favor because neither one would throw 7 during this extended period of throwing. Something is going to give to allow for this gap. That means the future shooters may have to throw a few 7s in a roll to compensate for these two good, long roll shooters. On average, if you keep the record straight, you will have accurate counting that the 7s would come out quite close to once in six throws. This is a natural occurrence, and you cannot avoid that.

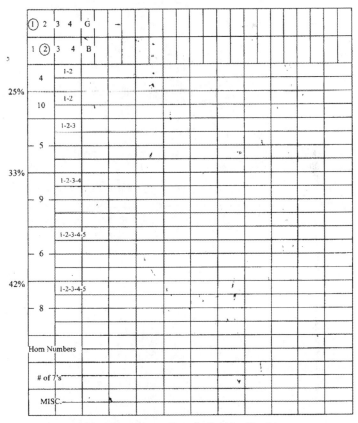

**Table 7. The Ultimate Form for Tracking Numbers**

Keeping track of the 7 in relationship with the overall number of throws is a critical method and is a good tool. What this tool calls for is that you should not play heavy until you have fully recouped part or all of all of your investment. It tells you to be careful, and that you must not continue playing this game forever and expect to win every time. It tells you when to exit the play or play with minimum bet, and when to play heavy. When you see that the 7 and the number of throws equal each other, you can be relaxed and start playing with a little aggression at first and later change your game plan. This is just a warning to you that at certain point for a number of throws, you must limit your bets, or will face with some damage later on.

# Chapter 4:
# Getting Good Data
# and Playing Well

This chapter is a continuing section on strategy and planning, so that you can play craps well. So far you have learned some basic things, such as keeping track of all point numbers (4, 5, 6, 8, 9, and 10) and the shooters. This chapter will show you how to track point numbers, the number of throws, and good and bad hands, with an emphasis on getting the most complete data possible.

For example, after a long roll or having gathered enough data for a whole table with full participation of ten players, your data is somewhat complete at that time. You can take a break or continue in data gathering; that is up to you to decide. If you collect enough information for twenty different shooters at the table, you have done a good job, and your data is ready to use from that point on. Sometimes I found that with a fewer number of players, the data did not come out correctly. If you try to record at least twenty players, you have done a good job, and your data is correct to use. You may even try to calculate the true percentage of each point number as compared to the right percentage for each, to see how your information is doing and what you intend to do next.

After that, you can make your plans as to which point numbers come out the most and which point numbers have not yet come out. You should pay attention to those point numbers that have not yet come out or are coming out the least often. You should play heavy on those numbers. For example, 4 has been thrown twenty times, and 10 had been thrown only ten times. You should play heavy on 10, and play with marginal bet on point 4 or do not play it at all. And you should play lightly on those point numbers that come out the most.

After reviewing Table 7, you should develop your own form to suit your taste and style. This is my ultimate form, which consists of all possibilities and even provides you with the calculations for the six point numbers in terms of the percentage for such pair numbers to appear in a given time. For example, you will expect pair point numbers 4 or 10 to come out 25 percent of the time and pair point numbers 6 and 8 to have a 42 percent chance to appear.

In this good table, perhaps you can include all horn bet numbers (2, 3, 11, 12) and the number of seven 7s, and a place for your miscellaneous bets—all as part of this form. You will use this form and revise it from time to time. Do not go the casino without it. It is a very important form, and do not let anyone get hold of it.

Table 10 is an adaptation of the ultimate form with tracks the point numbers and number of throws. You will see that under point number 4, this number has appeared three times during the recording process. For point number 10, this number has been thrown four times. Point number 5 has come up five times, and 9 appeared seven times. Finally, point number 6 appeared eight times, and point number 8 appeared ten times.

| | | | | | | | | | |
|---|---|---|---|---|---|---|---|---|---|
| ①②3④G | 00 | 0 | 0 | | (4 point numbers) | | | |
| 1 2 ③ 4 B | 0 | | | | (1 no point numbers) | | | |
| | | | | | | | | |
| 1-2-3<br>000 (3) | | | | | | | | |
| 1-2-3-4<br>0000 (4)<br>1-2-3-4 | | | | | | | | |
| 1-2-3-4-5<br>00000 (5) | | | | | | | | |
| 1-2-3-4-5-6-7<br>0000000 (7) | | | | | | | | |
| 1-2-3-4-5-6-7-8<br>00000000 (8) | | | | | | | | |
| 1-2-3-4-5-6-7-8-9-10<br>0000000000 (10) | | | | | | | | |

(row labels on left: —4—, —10—, —5—, —9—, —6—, —8—)

**Table 10. Tracking The Point Numbers & Number of Throws**

All the recording is confined to a certain time period. As you can see from Table 10, the times for point number 4 and point number 10 are very close. Then you look for the numbers for point number 5 and 9, and there is a difference of two, which shows you that 9 is slightly ahead of 5. And for points 6 and 8, there is a difference is two, which is not very much and can be considered as close as you can get. Sometimes after one complete cycle, or even two, your data will become more accurate. I assure you that your pair point numbers will come very close to each other after that many throws and for a long period, such as two to three hours of recording.

The collected data in this table is not sufficient for prediction purposes.

You must wait until you have collected enough good data before you can use that. As you can see, you only witnessed 4 come out three times, and 10 come out four times. For you to predict what the future will hold, you must wait until there are at least thirty to thirty-five times thrown for 6 and 8 combined, and with corresponding numbers thrown for the other remaining point numbers. By then you can honestly tell yourself that you have done a good job, and now you have enough good data to use for your prediction. Do not attempt to shortcut this method.

If you have collected enough data, you can conclude that certain point numbers have come out too often, and therefore other point numbers will be coming out in the future throws. For your own purpose, you must continue to keep track of all point numbers regardless of the time you spend at the table, and until sometime in the future you feel that you have enough data and quit. If you have enough data, you can assure yourself that you must concentrate on those point numbers that have yet to come out yet, and they will be coming out in the near future. That is your main objective.

Do you spend two or three hours of data gathering and then leave at the end of that time? Stay a little longer and be patient. You will be rewarded because you have been waited so long to get to this point. Make use of it and play some more and earn you money from this point on. Play heavy if you want to on those numbers that have yet to appear enough. Shy away from the overthrown numbers. Sometimes, these overthrown numbers still come out, but maybe not as often as before.

For the purpose of illustration, let us say that for 6 and 8, pair numbers, there are thirty throws for 6 and only twenty throws for 8. What do you do? You have collected enough good data, and you can make some logical conclusions. You should pay extra attention by playing 8, and pay little to no attention to 6. But you must not abandon 6 altogether. Sometimes, you still see 6 come out. You can use this method to make bets on the remaining four point numbers.

By doing it this way—knowing which point numbers come out the most and which point numbers come out the least—you can limit your liability and increase your chance of making a good profit. Pay attention to these kinds of throws, and especially pay attention to those point numbers that come out much less. Do yourself a favorite by calculating the percentage of outcome for your particular point number in mind; for example, there should be no greater than 25 percent for point numbers 4 or 10, and so on. If you do not keep track of this percentage from time to time, you may have been cheated, or you may even think that you have a good set of data to use, when in fact it is incorrectly collected for certain reasons. Therefore, you should do some periodic calculations on each pair of numbers to see just how good your data is and what you expect to gain from the information.

Sometimes you come to a table that is not too hot and not too cold—an even-play table. With Table 11, "Tracking Good Hands and Bad Hands," you have the chance to witness this kind of table, and it is a typical table you will encounter on a daily basis.

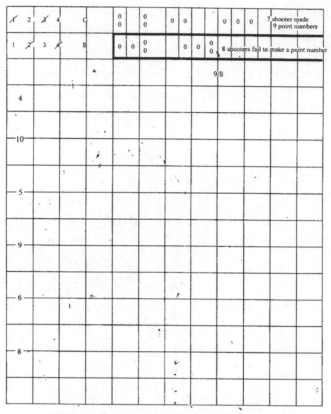

**Table 11. Tracking Good hands and Bad hands**

Note: This is a break even table because we have a 9 point numbers made vs. an 8 no point numbers made. be careful on this table.

To start your play, you must test the first four bets to see how good the table is performing and to see whether or not you should stay and continue playing. If you come out with even, then also track the good hands and the bad hands as indicated in Table 11. The good hands are shown on the very top line, and the bad hands are shown just below. We use a six-column table, with two rows for each type, labeled G for good hands and B for bad hands. As you can see from that table, a shooter made two point numbers, and this is recorded on the very top with two small circles for making the point numbers. Then came the bad shooter, who made no point number. This is shown just below, in the same column, with a small circle. Please remember that the top line represents just one shooter, and the bottom line can represent many shooters; just one circle is one shooter, and two circles represents two shooters.

In this case, the first shooter at the beginning of your record keeping, has made two point numbers. I used two small circles for that shooter. Then we will begin on the second shooter, who did not make a point number. Also, shooter number three did not make a point number. I use one small circle for shooter two and also one small circle for shooter three. Then I record shooter four, and that shooter threw two point numbers. You can see the two small circles as indicated on the top line in the third column.

Then I record shooters five and six, and both of these shooters did not make a point number. Then I continue to the seventh shooter and down to shooter number fifteen, the last shooter in this sample. I record the point numbers as they throw on Table 11, where you can see that there are seven good shooters and eight bad shooters. This is a break-even table, and you may even consider not playing in such a table. If you did play in this table, you probably will not come out ahead and may even lose a significant amount of money.

That is the main reason for you to keep track of all of the activities going on in your particular table at any given time. Time is important because it is the indicator as to how long you have kept recording the data. The longer you keep track, the better the data you get. Do not just keep track of the date for one hour and take a break and then later come back to record the same table again. If you are patient and consistent, you will be successful.

# CHAPTER 5:
## THE GAME OF CHANCE—
## PROBABILITY OUTCOMES

When you play craps, you should play it wisely and effectively. You must learn some facts about the game before you undertake such a task. You must master some basic rules and understand what percentage of time you can win and what percentage of time you can lose. If you make allowances for this error, then you are ready to play this game.

Table C-l, which is similar to Table C in chapter 2, uses a slightly different method to show the chance of winning any more point numbers after the first point number is made. We compare your chance of winning versus the casino's chance of winning.

## Table C—1 Your Chance of Winning vs. Casino Advantage

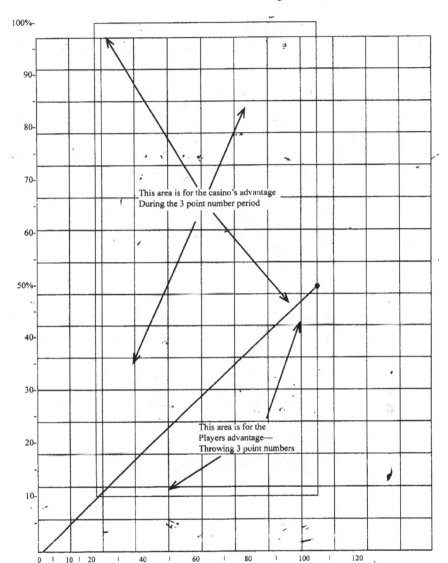

This area is for the casino's advantage
During the 3 point number period

This area is for the
Players advantage—
Throwing 3 point numbers

As you can see, your area is quite small as compared to the area occupied by the casino; the casino's area is three times as big. What is the meaning of this? It means your chance of winning any more point numbers after the first point number has been reduced. The house has three times the advantage over you—and on top of that, the number of point numbers made after the first three point numbers is no greater than 11%. You must play smart to beat the casino and play the opposite side of the game. Do not play the pass or come out lines. Instead, concentrate on the don't pass or don't come bets. From this table, I would expect you to play heavy after the first three point numbers come out. Do not be afraid of losing much because your winning chance is almost certain. But again, I must caution you that if the shooter throws two or three times to get a point number and does that again and again, you must stop playing the opposite side game. Instead you should play your normal and customary ways, the pass or come out lines. Please study the table carefully and see how it makes sense. Throughout my research period, I found that this was the most accurate table in the market because it represents the true and natural outcome of the game. Play the game to your heart's content and follow my methods.

# By the Numbers

This section explores the real probabilities in craps. Once you learn how to read your odds in the table, you will be ready to win some of the casino's money.

### Table 1: Probabilities Table

| Number | Number of ways to make this number | Dice combinations |
|:---:|:---:|:---:|
| 1 | 0 | None |
| 2 | 1 | 1:1 |
| 3 | 2 | 1:2; 2:1 |
| 4 | 3 | 1:3; 2:2; 3:1 |
| 5 | 4 | 1:4; 2:3; 3:2; 4:1 |
| 6 | 5 | 1:5; 2:4; 3:3; 4:2; 5:1 |
| 7 | 6 | 1:6; 2:5; 3:4; 4:3; 5:2; 6:1 |
| 8 | 5 | 2:6; 3:5; 4:4; 5:3; 6:2 |
| 9 | 4 | 3:6; 4:5; 5:4; 6:3 |

| 10 | 3 | 4:6; 5:5; 6:4 |
| 11 | 2 | 5:6; 6:5 |
| 12 | 1 | 6:6 |

There are only thirty-six different ways to throw these dices. To throw 6 and 8 compared to 7 is 10/6 =1.67 times better odds than throwing a 7.

To throw 5 and 9 compared to a 7 is 8/6 = 1.33 times better odds than throwing a 7.

In order for you to benefit from this outcome, bet two point numbers instead of one at a time. But of course you also are facing the probability of throwing a 7 before throwing your numbers. You are thinking that your two numbers are better than just a single number, and that is the reason you make this kind of play. It is a proper and acceptable method, providing that you take down the throw point number, the 6 or 8, one at a time, in order to come out ahead. If you leave these two bets along, after you get back just one of these two, and the shooter has already thrown six times, the chance of throwing a 7 before your point number is greater, and you are at greater risk from this point on. Therefore you should play conservatively and maybe just take one of these numbers down and leave the other point number alone. If you can do that, you will come out ahead of the game.

From Table 1, you can see that you have thirty-six different ways to make a number

But you cannot throw the number 1 under any circumstance. As you can see, there are more 7s than any other numbers. We often call this kind of table the bell curve table. This is because if you are plotting these numbers on a graph, with the numbers or point numbers on bottom from left to right, and you plot the number of ways to make any of these numbers using the vertical axis, it forms a bell. As you can see below, the left side will exactly match the right side. What this mean is that each paired set of point numbers—4 and 10, 5 and 9, 6 and 8—can be made in the same number of ways. For example, Table 1 shows there are three ways to make each of the point numbers 4 and 10. As you reach the middle of Table 1, you see you have the best chance of beating the house by playing on both 6 and 8, or both 5 and 9, at the same time, compared to any other pair numbers.

This is so because you have a better chance to hit one of these two numbers than just playing with one number. As you go down the curve, to point numbers 5 and 9 for example, your chance of getting either of these two numbers before a 7 comes out is better by 33 percent.

If you play by pure probability, without regard to the numbers of throws already made, your chance of getting a 7 out is much greater than getting back your total investment. By virtue of this table, when you bet on just 8, the house has a 13 percent advantage over you. As you go further down the bell curve, to point number 4 for example, you have a 50 percent of getting that number. But if you did get that number, you have an almost two-for-one advantage over the house for your money, and that is a very good return. You still have to pay the house a 5 percent commission, which is not bad.

From my previous chapters, you have learned how to use my form to record the outcome of all the shooters at that table. You have also learned how to recognize a hot and cold table. If you recently observed a very hot shooter, I can assure you he will not do well when the dice later return for this hot shooter to throw again. I guarantee you that this same hot shooter will not do as well as before and may only throw just one point number or none. This is partly due to the probability table in which the good hands must equal the number of bad hands, to even out, on the average, for all of the previous throws. In the end, there will be no gain and no loss. This is part of the bell curve system, and it is natural for all things to come to an equilibrium stage.

Do not expect miracles, and do not expect the same hot shooter to throw many point numbers again. Beware of this criteria, pay attention, and do not attempt to play heavy. Tables 2 and 3 reinforce what you learned from Table C in chapter 2. You can see that there is a huge and sudden drop from the time you make the first point number to the end of the third point number. You still have high hope of making these three numbers with a combined chance of 80 percent, though you have less than an 11 percent chance of making the third point number. The area beyond point number three gets harder and harder.

Do not expect to win very much in the remaining area, because point numbers four to nine are very hard to get. During my thirty years of playing craps, I have not seen anyone shoot nine point numbers. I have seen shooters make eight numbers on two occasions, and both of these events occurred in the Las Vegas area back in 2008 and 2009. I have seen five point numbers on many occasions. Throwing point number six is very difficult, and only a few shooters can make it to this point.

When a shooter makes these high point numbers, she often makes the point numbers in a very quick manner. She may throw two or three times, and a point number appears. Later, at the beginning of a new game, she may throw a 7 first and then later a point number. But this quick throw of point numbers is repeated again and again. This same shooter would not be able to make long roll throws. After a few throws comes a point number. This process would take place until the shooter makes her last point number. The shooter was throwing for more than five or six times, and then out came a 7. The game is over for this shooter.

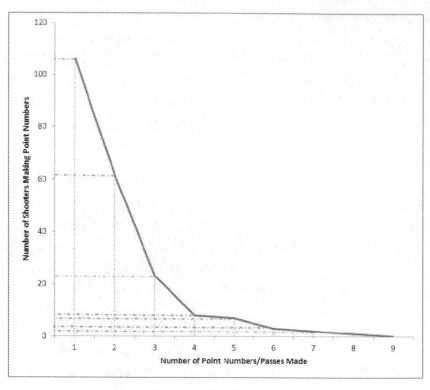

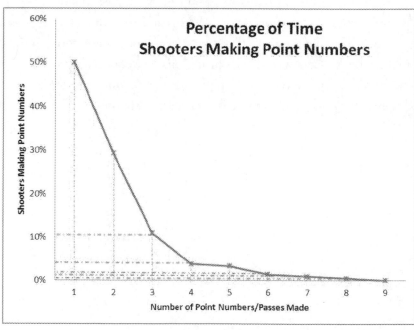

Before you decide to play this game, please take a look at Table 4 and study it carefully. This table shows your chance of winning and your chance of losing in craps. As you can see, the best chance for you to win is by betting pass line/come bet with the maximum odds allowed by the casino. You can also play the don't pass/don't come with maximum odds. Under these conditions, you give up less than a 1 percent advantage to the house. This is the best you can get compared to any other casino table or slot machine games.

If you just play the game without any odds on the pass line, for example, the house has a slight edge over you. You have an advantage over the house because you place odds on these bets. The next good bet is the don't pass/don't come bets, with maximum lays. You have a better outcome by doing it this way.

There are several ways to play this game—but only a few ways are correct ways. Therefore you must place maximum odds on the pass line and come out lines. Next, you can play the pass line/come line and no odds, but the house still has a slight advantage over you with no odds, less than 2 percent in favor of the house. This is not a proper way to play this game. Finally you can play the place bets for 6 and 8. All these bets should give you a better opportunity to win some money, but only if you play both of the pair numbers at the same time.

As you go down to this table and into other kinds of betting, such as any craps, hard ways, and any 7, your chance of winning gets worst. Do not put your money in these types of bets because they do not give you a better return for your money. Concentrate on the following: pass line/come bet with odds, don't pass/don't come with maximum lays. These bets should give you a favorable return on your money. Other bets are wasting your money and should be avoided at all costs. Look at Table 4 closely: the worst bet is by playing any 7, a 16.70 percent chance for the house.

### Table 4: Your Bets against the House Advantage

| Bet | House Edge (Percent) |
| :---: | :---: |
| Pass Line/Come Bet | 1.41 |
| Don't Pass/Come | 1.40 |
| Pass line/Come Bet 2X odds | 0.85 |

| Don't Pass/Come 2X odds | 0.83 |
|---|---|
| Place 6 and 8 | 1.52 |
| Place 5 and 9 | 4.00 |
| Place 4 and 10 | 6.67 |
| Buy 6 or 8 | 4.76 |
| Buy 5 or 9 | 4.76 |
| Buy 4 or 10 | 4.76 |
| Lay 6 or 8 | 4.00 |
| Lay 5 or 9 | 3.23 |
| Lay 4 or 10 | 2.44 |
| Field Bet | 5.56 |
| Any Craps | 11.11 |
| Hard Way 6 or 8 | 9.09 |
| Hard Way 4 or 10 | 11.10 |
| 11 or 3 | 11.10 |
| 2 or 12 | 13.90 |
| Any 7 | 16.70 |

Remember Table 10 in chapter 4, when you learned how to record all the numbers come out, such as the point numbers 4, 5, 6, 8, 9, and 10, a total of six point numbers? At certain times, such as at the end of the complete go around of a table of seven to ten players, you counted that there are a total of ten shooters to throw these dices. You will do certain math calculation at that time to see how the table is performing and how well you have done so far. This math calculation is very simple and handy to use, so do not be discouraged by using this simple math. It is quite easy to learn.

Table 6 shows the so-called calculation of possible outcome for all the numbers. To begin with, at the end of a full round of the table, you might have recorded that ten shooters in your table had thrown a total of twenty-seven times for the number 4 and twenty-nine times for the number 10. For numbers 5 or 9, you witnessed a total throw of thirty-five times for either of these two numbers. Finally, you recorded a total of forty-five times for 6 and forty-seven times for 8. From these figures, you will calculate the percentage of each of the pairs by taking an average of the two numbers. See Table 10 for detailed calculations.

I have accumulated three sets of data, and they are recorded in Table 6. For the second set of data, I recorded a total of thirty-four times for 4 or 10, forty-two times for 5 or 9, and finally fifty-three times for 6 or 8. As you can see from this table, in the third column the actual throws are shown herein. From there, I recorded three different outcomes with three different results, but all were within the required range. For example, in set one there are 107 throws, and in set two I recorded a total of 129 throws. Finally, I recorded a total of 63 throws with various outcomes that appeared on the table. From these results, I have calculated the percentage of each pair of the point numbers, such as 4 or 10, in the first column. From the first column, you will find there is a 25 percent outcome for these two point numbers. You will see that there is a 33 percent outcome for 5 or 9. Finally, there is a 42 percent outcome for 6 or 8. The next columns will yield a slightly different outcome. Then from this data, I have used the average number of these three sets of data. The result is shown on the table.

In the middle of Table 6, you will see the summary data for all the throws. I use a range for each pair of the point numbers. For example, for pair 4 and 10, the range is 25–27 percent. The range for pair 5 and 9 is 33–35 percent. Finally, I come across a range of 38–42 percent for pair 6 and 8.

**Table 6:- Calculation of Percentage for Certain Point Number**

| Point Number | # of Point Number | % | # of Point Number | % | # of Point Number | % |
|---|---|---|---|---|---|---|
| 4 or 10 | 27 | 25 | 34 | 26 | 17 | 27 |
| 5 or 9 | 35 | 33 | 42 | 33 | 22 | 35 |
| 6 or 8 | 45 | 42 | 53 | 41 | 24 | 38 |
| | 107 | | 129 | | 63 | |

### Summary of These Throws

| Point Numbers | Range of these Numbers |
|---|---|
| 4 or 10 | 25–27% |
| 5 or 9 | 33–35% |
| 6 or 8 | 38–42% |

### Actual Percentage from Probability Table

| Point Numbers | Number of Ways of the Numbers | % |
|---|---|---|
| 4 or 10 | 6 | 25 |
| 5 or 9 | 8 | 33 |
| 6 or 8 | 10 | 42 |
| | 24 Ways | 100% |

From the probability table, Table 1, I calculate the total number of ways to make a pair point number, 4 or 10. I then calculate how many different ways of making 5 or 9, and I use the same method to calculate how many different ways of making 6 or 8. From those calculations I come up with a twenty-four ways in which to make all these three pair point numbers. I finally calculate the actual percentage of each of the pair point numbers. There is a 25 percent chance of making these pair point numbers, 4 or 10, out of the total throws in a given time in a given table. There is a 33 percent chance of making 5 or 9. Finally, there is a 42 percent chance of making 6 or 8. The sum of this is equal to 100 percent.

Because this is the actual outcome for each pair of numbers, I use this as my model to check how close my actual research data is, compared to this true outcome expectation

To my surprise, they are very close. See for yourself in Table 6: the top portion of my research data comes up very close to the actual outcome as predicted by the probability theory. Therefore, when you do your recording, you must also do some simple math calculation from time to time, just to check your method and provide yourself with confidence to play this game in the right manner.

What is important from this observation is that you can play with confidence if you know that your figure is within the range. If you find that your outcome numbers are in excess of the average thrown numbers allowed, this will give you an indicator or signal that you are in a danger zone. Do not play with those point numbers. You should be paying more attention to the numbers with a below-average outcome.

Table 6 is a very powerful tool, and it is up to you to keep up with your good habit of maintaining an accurate record on all throws for the shooters at your table.

For example, if you do not have this table, you are gambling in a blind alley, and you have no way of knowing exactly where you are at any given point. You are playing this game just like everyone else in the table. You must maintain a positive attitude: you are here to win, and you are going to keep accurate records on all counts. Do not let your friends talk you out of it; let them play in their usual way. But you are different because you have acquired a new technique, and it is working. Test my method to see if you agree.

# Chapter 6:
# Exit Plan

Up to this point, you have learned some of my potent and secret methods of playing craps the correct way. Once you have mastered my techniques, use and test them to see whether or not you can improve them. Perhaps you should use a combination of these methods to achieve your goal. When I first arrive at a table, I stay there to observe the first two shooters to see how well they perform. Are they making point numbers? I need to know before I play this game. I do not waste my hard-earned dollars or give it away without a fight. If the table is good, I will play the normal hands, pass lines, or come out lines. Otherwise, I will wait or play the opposite way, don't pass or don't come line bets, with maximum lays on each. Sometimes I wait for the full table, with at least seven players, before I play. I usually go from casino to casino until I find such a table to play my kind of game. I do not just go to any table and start my game—I wait for my opportunity. I will take my time to find the right table, because I want to win and do not just give away my money to the casino.

I have played this game for over thirty years, and I win more often than I lose. Sometimes I have neglected my own advice by not using the hit and run approach to play my game. When you play the solid gold chain method, be prepared to exit at any moment. Perhaps you should walk away after a long thrown hand, and you are winning with a good sum of money. You should never stay at a given table for an extended period of time after a very solid performance. Do not expect and anticipate that the sky is the limit—what goes up can go down much more quickly. Look at the stock market as an example. When you win a couple hundred dollars from the casino, you should be content and satisfied with what you have. Set up a gambling principal to remind you that you must exit from a table once you have won about two hundred dollars. This is the casino's money, not your initial investment. If you stay at the table any longer, you might lose all the money you won thus far, plus some of your own money. This is not your style. You must play to win. You will do better than the other players who have refused to leave the table once they won some of the casino's money. Be kind to yourself and be ready to hit the road once you are ahead of the game; just win a small sum and be happy. Do not stay long and expect that you are invincible and cannot be beaten. Then you will think that you have learned all the secret methods that cannot be broken. Self-control is a virtue and is the most prudent method to play this game the right way. Be kind to yourself, take a short break, and walk away and relax after a winning hand. If you follow my methods, you would be a much better player because you have learned my rules and are able to control your winning habit.

# PART II:
# CRAPS AND THE CASINO

# CHAPTER 7:
# HISTORY OF CRAPS

The origin of dice as we know it can be traced back to the ancient times, where fortunate tellers and medicine men used to throw certain objects such as sticks, stones, sacred arrows, bones, rocks, and other items to the ground to predict future events. Then changes were made through the use of various forms, shapes, sizes, and markings, and dice became used as gambling tools. These dice were original made of stones, woods, bones, animal teeth, and sometimes horns, nutshells, and seeds. Cubical dice were used in early Egypt around 630 BC. Dice were also used by American Indians and in the early Arab world. In the Roman and Greek eras, dice were made of expensive materials such as ivory, precious stones and metals, or porcelain. Roman emperors Augustine, Nero, and Caligula were considered devoted dice players. Modem dice are made of a very hard, chemical materials full of cellulose. Dice edges are very flat and smooth, and the comers are well balanced to give that certain unbiased roll so that the landing is random.

Dice games themselves are thousands of years old. One version of the origin of craps has its beginning in AD 1125, during the Third Crusade. As the story goes, Sir William of Tyre and his loyal crusaders came to a place known as Asart, or Hazarth. There they encountered a fierce fight at the enemy's castle. To take advantage of such conditions, they laid siege to the castle and later settled there. They spent their time enjoying a game they called Hazard, which was based on the name of the castle. That game was later modified and became craps as we know it.

Some scholars believed that game was developed long before Hazard. It is believed that Arabic empires employed the dice game called Al Zar, meaning dice, and it came from there and later migrated to Europe in the twelfth century.

In any case, Hazard was brought to the Americas by the first English setters on the *Mayflower* journey. Later these settlers built homes in the New England states. English Hazard was very popular in New Orleans in the 1800s, and the French people called it "Crap." Then came variations of the game that were simpler and faster. It became a table game in the nineteenth century; at that time, various forms of numbers were introduced, such as 6 and 8, field numbers, win and come bids, and place and pass line bids. The game became popular and was often played at riverboats on the Mississippi, as well as throughout the rest of the country. In 1931 casino gaming was legalized in the state of Nevada, and casino craps became very popular all over the world.

Then came a person named John H Winn, who perfected the game and made many changes, including allowing players to bet right and wrong. He introduced some extra space in the crap table to allow for "don't pass" or "don't come" bets. Mr. Winn's invention was credited as the father of modern craps. He devised certain craps rules that the modem casinos are still using today.

In the 1990s, slot machines overtook craps as number one. However, casino and Internet craps remain very popular.

# CHAPTER 8:
# KINDS OF CRAPS TABLES IN DIFFERENT CASINOS

The current craps table is quite new. It has been modified many times since its invention in 1950 by John H Winn. Each casino has a slightly different table, but the basic layout is the same, such as the pass line, come out bet line, field bets, horn bets, hard number bets, don't pass and don't come bets, and more. For example, most of Harrah's tables are similar in size, but the tables at the Harrah's of Las Vegas are much longer than at other Harrah's locations. The main items in these table are still the same. Each table has the same "fire bet" designation, in the front of each player, numbering 1 to 14.

Some casino tables have "Big 6 and 8" on them, whereas others do not have this designation. Some tables have the bet called "Hop the Number." You have to find a table that suits your taste.

When you to go to some of the local Indian casinos, the rules of playing are very different.

You still have the pass line and come out bets, hard numbers, and others with similar layout as other casinos. But you have a little chance of throwing the dices to get what you want. There is no way for you to set the dices before throwing them. Controlled dice throwing does not exist. If you are used to this kind of throwing the dice, then the Indian casinos are not for you. In several Indian casinos, you use two dices and throw these to the opposite side of the table as you normally would. There are two possible outcomes: a red or blue number will appear. These red and blue boxes are located next to the automatic machine, just the front of the stickman. The stickman uses the automatic machine to pick two cards on a random basis. These two cards will be placed in the red and blue boxes. Then the stickman places one card on the left and one card on the right, which represent red or blue box. If the shooter throws the higher number of the two—say 2 and 1 appear, and 2 is the higher number of the two, and it is the ted color—then the stickman will open the card under the red side of the two boxes. He then reads it out to get a number, horn numbers or point numbers, or any other numbers to correspond to the throw number. If the players place bets in that number—the red box number, for example—the dealer will pay that person for that bet in accordance with the proper payoff. Then the shooter will continue to throw until he throws of point number or sevens out. The process will continue to the next player or shooter around the table.

This process is solely controlled by the arbitrary or by the random throwing method. The Indian casinos do not want you to win very often; they want to see that all outcome numbers will have an equal chance and are solely based on the probability curve. If you prefer a conventional method, this game is not for you. There are not too many player that like to play at such a table due to its usual nature of throwing the dices to get a number. Most people prefer a live throwing process where you throw a number, and if you bet on that number, then you will get paid. The Indian process is based on random throwing, and the good hands are usually not equal to the bad hands. If you use my recording method, you would encounter more bad hands than good hands. If you play the game correctly, you could still win some by paying attention to those point numbers that come out less often and will likely come out in the next few throws.

When an Indian casino in Lincoln, California, called the Thunder Valley Casino and Resort, opened in 2007, the craps table was at one point run by an automatic machine. It now has a stickman and dealers and a boxman. The minimum bet is only $5 per hand.

I have checked the various Indian Casinos and found that there is no such thing as a "normal" kind of craps table; they all have the same or similar system, where you do not get the number you throw out as your point number. Instead, the thrown number corresponds to the higher of the two numbers with either a red color or a blue color.

The Indian casinos appear to use a much different approach to tackle craps, and they do not intend to lose much by using this ironclad method. I do not like it, and it is not a practical method. It destroys the traditional method of craps, which is very old and should not be changed to where a machine selects the point numbers. This method does not give one a joy or the challenge of being a good craps shooter. That is the main reason that they have only one such table in any given casino at this time: not many players will enjoy playing in such an environment. I suggest that they change their method of playing back to the traditional method, using a live shooter to throw the point numbers. They are not going to modify their method, so you should avoid playing at such tables or casino at all costs. After all, you have many choices, so why should you go to a place in which they control your game and tell you what to do and how they want you to play it?

I believe that the correct way to play craps is by natural throw and letting nature takes its course. Whatever the throw number comes out, you expect 50 percent of the time to win and 50 percent of the time to lose, if you are using the controlled dice throwing method discussed in chapter 13. With a completely random and natural throw, you will have a slight disadvantage, and your chance of winning or throwing one point number is actually less than 50 percent. But this is still better than slot machines. For this reason, you should concentrate your main effort on a large, customary throwing table, such as Las Vegas, to play this exciting game.

I have not used any Indian casino data in my research project because they are not representative of the game in general due to the method of throwing the dice and the reading them afterward. This is unorthodox and is not suitable for most players. If you like the excitement and shouting and yelling and have good time, go to the large casinos and enjoy the atmosphere.

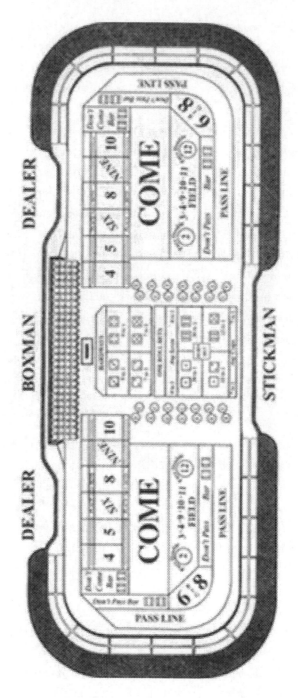

*The Changing World: Improvement in Table Construction*

The building of a craps table is challenging, and yet you do not need to do that because you can buy one at a closed-down casino. In 2008, you could purchase such a table in Reno at the Flamingo Casino for a fair price, a few hundred dollars. You will still have a chance to get such a table soon because there will be lots of smaller casinos that will be out of business. Look for this type of deal in the future.

After such a purchase, you will have a practical way of testing the controlled dice method at your home to see whether or not it is working. But you still have to spend an enormous amount of time practicing the techniques on a daily basis.


The craps table is usually made up with hardwood materials on the bottom and a soft foam on the top; in the old days, this was the main focus in building a good table. Then some skill shooters gained a broad knowledge by using such a table and did very well on the game, concentrating their throw on certain part of the table and then causing their dices to land in a certain way to arrive at a particular number for a wining hand.

Soon this information was passed on to the casino industry, prompting them to look for a better design. A change to the design for a better table was imminent. The new design called for certain kinds of hardwood boards be placed on the bottom with certain types of foam on top. That design did not go well and was used for a short period; later the industry made some modifications, and it became what it is today.

The craps table today is made up with solid hardwood materials and filled with soft felt on top. The two sides where the stickman and boxman are located are installed with a solid piece of mirrors or solid glass on both sides. The back side, the long opposite sides just adjacent to the two dealers, or the end of numbers 4 and 10, are made up with solid foams with cubes or cones squarely in between and spaced a certain way to reflect the throwing dices to land a certain way. This practice is to allow for free throwing or random numbers throwing to occur. The house is not very happy to see shooters using a controlled dice method because this process will take up more time, and the house loses more money in any downtime. The casino wants to keep the dices moving and wants the players to make mistakes so that the house will win and a make profit. They make these cones with solid rubber materials, squarely spaced with just the tips pointing certain ways, and this construction causes the dice to bounce and land in an arbitrary way, instead of landing in the shooter's desired way.

There is no such thing as standard craps table. Each casino is allowed to build its own craps table to suit its own decor and need. There are no rules or regulations governing what is considered a proper way to construct the table. It is left to the individual casino to decide what style they need. The table height and width, the chip rack setting with certain construction and materials, the kinds of railings, the height of the walls and types of fillings—these are all relative. It is believed that each casino can choose the size of the rubber pyramids, the layout, the kinds of materials used to build it, and other design considerations. I'd like the casino to take out all the cubes or cones from each end, because these areas are danger zones for throwing purposes.

Craps table comes in various sizes. Most of the casinos use a size of twelve or fourteen feet for their favorite tables. Most of the craps tables at Harrah's Casino are twelve feet. However, you may encounter few casinos using a ten-foot long table, which is called a mini plates table. My research found these smaller tables, as well as some tables a few inches over twelve feet, and there were some in between. I have not found two exactly sized tables in two different casinos. Each has a few inches more or less than the others.

Construction materials used to build a good craps table vary from one casino to another, but most of them use the top materials such as hardwood mahogany with solid stains all around, and semi-soft felt on top of the table. There are some casinos using synthetics instead of felt due to its cost and looks. Synthetics last longer but oftentimes cause certain shooters to overthrow the dices and land outside the table. This is due to the smooth surface that causes the dices to slide faster than one built with felt materials.

The perfect craps table needs added volara foam or other synthetic materials underneath the felt for smooth throwing. On table's bottom is often called the layout, "floorette," simply the bottom. This bottom is often elevated about twenty-eight inches off the floor, the so-called regulation height that is standard for all casinos.

Each casino can have different betting areas appear on the table, but they have same or similar features. All craps tables have the pass line winding around the outside of the layout, with don't pass bet areas just above it. Then you have the field box numbers 2, 3, 4, 9, 10, 11, and 12, just above the don't pass line. The come area is located in approximately the same location for all casinos, just above the field box numbers and just below the point numbers of 4, 5, 6, 8, 9, and 10, which are at the top of the layout. Some casinos do not want to spend extra money to print their own letterings, and they purchase a preprinted floorette instead.

Some craps table bottom will feature boxes for miscellaneous hop bets at the top of the hard ways boxes, and a few casinos have tables with craps and 11 boxes rolling down either side of the proposition bets. Some casinos offer big 6 and big 8, and others offer none; this is not a standard procedure. Look for a table you like to play and concentrate your effort.

# CHAPTER 9:
# THE STATE OF THE STRIP

The gambling industry had a difficult time of making a decent profit in 2010. Many of the older casinos may be facing closure in the near future. In the last two years, Las Vegas has added two mega-sized casinos, including the City Center Casino and Resort and the Aria at City Center Las Vegas, located on the Strip. Another gigantic block-long casino, named The Cosmopolitan of Las Vegas, had the grand opening on December 31, 2010.

According to Moody's Financial Report, the gambling industry has not fully recovered from the prolonged recession, which affected every section of the economy. It is anticipated the turnaround will occur in early 2012. The casinos' financial condition is now listed as stable condition. They are not in a healthy state, but many of the casinos have invested large sums of capital in recent years. They are facing large debts and that must be paid down shortly. This will affect their overall book in the short term. They have a long way to go before Moody can change its rating in this industry from stable to a positive mode.

There are certain gambling locations that do better than the others. The gambling revenues are up 7 percent for the first quarter of 2010 for those casinos located on the Las Vegas Strip. But this is not necessary the trend for the rest of 2010. In fact, it is estimated that the revenue for the remaining three quarters will remain flat. Some believe the bottom has been reached and there could be a turn around in the coming years. Other regions in the eastern part of the country are doing just as well. But revenue for the Atlantic City area has not been improved due to competition from neighboring states. Part of the decline in revenue is due to a reduction of discretionary consumer spending and the periodic payments of debt services.

Most of the Indian casinos in the California area are doing quite well. Some of them added more hotel and casino areas, and a few of them are cutting down on permanent staff to save costs. Overall their balance sheets show a good return for their invested capital compared to the owners in the Las Vegas areas.

# CHAPTER 10:
# CASINO SECURITY SYSTEMS
# AND MONITORING SYSTEMS

Today all casinos have installed similar kinds of security and monitoring systems. These systems require around-the–clock, in-house monitoring and personnel patrolling the casino areas. These systems work quite well and are able to detect any types of cheaters patrons in the playing area who are having medical problems. There are various types of in-house monitoring and security systems, and each casino can change the system to be suitable for their needs.

All alarms and events from multiple detection systems and from individual devices themselves can be monitored and recorded by the casino central system. Any wireless transmitters can be seamlessly woven into the casino security network for both device monitoring and mobile personal duress pendants. For emergency calls, casino security personal usually carry a wireless set in their pocket. Other wireless transmitters may be used to monitor doors, motion detectors, glass-break detectors, and other equipment.

A software scheduler will ignore alarms during user-specified time windows. The scheduler can be used to turn relays on and off in order to control lights, equipment, intercoms, or other applications. Other facility security systems such as fire alarm panels can be integrated to provide instant notification and description of the location over handheld, two-way radios.

Each casino uses closed-circuit television cameras that are positioned throughout the casino area; the cameras may be displaced in roving staff vehicles or on a hand-carried video receiver. Any cameras may be called up for view automatically as the result of an alarm event, or they can be manually checked at the discretion of the staff.

Each casino is equipped with a team of skilled monitoring personnel in the main office, closely reviewing floor activity. This team member is not just looking out for potential gambling cheaters but is also paying closer attention to dealers who have access to large amounts of chips and may take advantage of the system by stealing from the table.

Some kinds of mild cheating is okay. The house might leave you alone if you have not caused too much damage or won too much. Take card counting. Although counting cards on one hand is not illegal, a good card counter in blackjack gains a statistical advantage over the house. If the casino knows of this, and if you have won many times in a row with large sums of money, the casino will not let you keep winning. Soon you will be escorted out of the casino and may not be allowed to come back later to play the same game.

Card counting teams from MIT made millions off Las Vegas and have since been immortalized in a book and film. The MIT team's innovation was to have separate roles for certain players. For example, some were there to count and place small bets, and others acted as high rollers and made big bets when the decks were favorable. It is quite easy to detect such players; their system is based betting patterns, lots of small bets followed by some big ones. This MIT team performed better and longer than any previous card-counting team in history. They survived longer because each member had a different role, and that separation of duties gave the appearance of legitimate betting patterns.

The following are a few examples of cheating the casinos as captured by video camera. There are many ways the players can shift the odds in their favor but appear to be legitimate.

The infinite hundred–dollar-bill could easily cheat the casino slot machines. One team walked off with over $1.2 million from a casino without too much trouble. The casino later determined that a new hundred-dollar bill could be fed into a certain slot machine, and if you hit the button at just the right time, the machine would give the player $100 in credit while spitting the actual bill right back into the player's hands.

The chip cup case involved some high-dollar chips hiding underneath a stack of $5 chips, appearing like a roll of solid $5 chips. Because the dealer and player are working together, the player would ask the dealer to change his hundred-dollar bill by switching these chips. According to a later testimony from the dealer, this process had been going on for some time. The casino lost a great sum of the money due to this arrangement.

A player palms a card and trades it with a neighbor to make a better blackjack hand. This trick is decidedly low tech, but it is nearly undetectable when done with great skill.

The programmer who worked on a video poker game snuck in some code that produced an automatic royal flush if a player followed a specific sequence of betting over the course of seven or eight hands.

All facilities have security concerns unique to their environment. Casinos tend to have a broader set of security issues than many other settings. Casinos are entertainment centers, hotels, and restaurants, and they possess a substantial amount of cash at their cashing center. A primary factor that contributes to these potential dangers is that at any given time, a casino is often extremely crowded. Massive crowds are a concern because the more people in an area, the more likely something is going to happen. This could be an assault, a group of thieves looking for an easy target, or an accident that may have been prevented or detected if there were fewer people present. Casinos have developed specific ways to help reduce the likelihood of these events occurring; they also find ways to detect any potentially detrimental concern before it becomes a major problem. However, if all of these fail, they have developed strategies to handle the issue to the best of their abilities.

The primary goal of any security officer or surveillance officer in a casino is the same as in virtually any other facility: to protect the visitors, employees, and assets of the organization. Because this role is so vitally important, both of these security positions are very detailed about what their job entails, as well as what their qualifications must be. A security officer's main responsibilities include patrolling the area, inspecting anything suspicious, enforcing the casino's rules, handling emergency situations, and escorting anyone transporting chips.

A surveillance officer has a more behind-the-scenes job. Duties include monitoring CCTV cameras, videotaping and observing activities around the casino, and identifying any suspicious activity. Questionable activity may include a host of various behaviors, and it may be indicative of employee embezzlement, cheating at the games, stealing from patrons, or attempted fraud. Due to the critical nature of tile surveillance position, it has a more extensive list of requirements. Each officer should have training in the fields of casinos dealers and background dealing with casino games such as slots machines, craps, poker, and various other games.

All security officers must be aware of anything that could cause harm to an individual in the future, even if it appears to be harmless at the moment. Seeing a potential safety hazard and assuming someone else will fix it could mean that the problem will not be taken care of until an accident occurs. If an officer realizes that something could be a potential safety hazard, he must either fix the problem himself or find someone else who can.

Unfortunately, all accidents are not real accidents—some are an attempt to defraud the casino. Although it is more common for someone attempting to file a fraudulent lawsuit to be a customer, occasionally an employee will have an accident and collect workman's compensation. CCTV cameras arc used to capture an accident on videotape that has obviously been faked, giving the plaintiff no legal grounds to sue for negligence or getting workman's compensation benefits.

Fires are a major risk in any casino. Enormous amounts of people frequent casinos on a daily basis, and the noise levels are also extremely high, making it difficult to hear in the event a fire alarm activates. The noise may include people talking, bells going off, and background music. To avoid unnecessary false fire alarms, certain safety measures are also taken into account, including a twenty-second time delay for all smoke detectors. This means the central alarm system is given a signal before the actual alarm goes off on the floor, giving them time to investigate if there is actually a fire.

Another major concern is the criminal activity that takes place on casino floors. This includes fraud, theft, and gambling schemes, many of which arc felonies. There are many types of casino thefts and crimes. Some of these crimes are committed by employees who are trying to cash in extra bucks from their employer, claiming that they are underpaid. Employee embezzlement is a very serious issue in a casino environment, with its readily available cash on hand. Some employees have no choice but to steal a few chips at the beginning, and later on that activity turns into a major crime. First some employees will steal alone by pocketing chips; others may work in collusion with an outsider to cheat the casino. Popular forms of theft perpetrated by outside thieves include purse snatching, stealing wallets, and switching. Switching is when someone chooses a mark that appears to have a large amount of cash or other valuables with them and is carrying a similar item, such as a briefcase or suitcase. The thief will casually switch the expensive item with the similar item, which is less valuable and filled with rocks or newspaper.

There are far too many forms of gambling schemes to cheat the casino. The most popular of these are stringing, distraction schemes, and manipulation of the cards.

Stringing is where a customer takes a coin and inserts a piece of fishing line into it, to retrieve it from the machine. The line is then wrapped around their finger to keep yo-yoing the coin into a slot machine for repeated use. Distraction may occur when some other patrons distract an employee or the dealer, and then someone changes a bet to the cheater's favor. This process can happen solely by the cheater or in collusion with an employee or dealer who is running the game. For a blackjack game, the cards may be marked with a special letter not readily detected by the casino camera. Another method is to manipulate the cards with a false shuffle, stacking the deck to allow an outside partner to know which card is being played.

Other criminal activities casinos have to dealt with are related to assaults and robberies, sometimes at gunpoint. This happens when the casino cage is filled with tons of cash at the beginning of the month. An assault in a casino is often a combination of aggression over losing a substantial amount of money, as well as people using illegal drugs and drinking excessively.

There was a famous criminal case that occurred in 1997 in which two eighteen-year-old California boys visiting the Primadona Resort (now called the Primm Valley Casino) murdered and raped a seven-year-old girl. This was a devastating story for the casino industry. This girl came with her fourteen-year-old brother and her father. When she went to the restroom, her family members went somewhere else to wait for her. She later was raped and strangled by these two California boys. At that time of the murder, no one knew this had happened. Her family members thought she went back to the hotel room and waited for them. They did not take the time to trace her and look for her. Later, someone discovered her body in the restroom, in the early morning hours.

This accident occurred because the father was too busy playing the slots machines, and her brother was elsewhere looking for something to buy to take home. Her father later claimed that his daughter was never out of his sight except for a brief period. However, security reports show that the girl had been found wandering around the casino unsupervised at least three different times on the night the murder occurred. Additionally, the father had been warned repeatedly about not supervising his daughter while he was playing the slot machines.

This tragic event took place with the CCTV cameras recording the moments leading to the child's death. At that time, the technology was not quite advance, and CCTV cameras were not very reliable. The casino security personnel did not know that the pictures captured in the CCTV cameras were accurate, and they were unable to interpret exactly what was in the images. The truth of the matter was that one boy followed the girl right into the bathroom while the other watching outside the bathroom insured no one would get in to witness the killing. Later on, the dead girl's mother claimed that the casino personnel did not provide adequate security for her daughter.

CCTV cameras are an essential element of casino security. By using the pan, tilt, and zoom features, CCTV cameras can monitor a relatively large area without the extra expense of needing additional cameras and other security personnel on-site. They can capture an unarguable image of cheating, embezzlement, and assault. If such technology was employed in 1997, the murder could have been prevented. As it was, though, the camera images assisted in identifying and convicting the murderer, who in 1998 was sentenced to four life terms in prison.

# Chapter 11:
# Special Offers and Promotions

When you play in any casino for the very first time, the casino promotion manager actively seeks to enlist you to be a favored customers by offering you certain benefits. They may offer you certain bonus points when you first play at their casino. Before you come to play at that casino, you may have received an invitation from them, full of freebies and possibly worth hundreds of dollars in casino chips or free plays, and coupons worth certain casino values that are good for certain types of games.

If you go there and play some casino games with a decent amount on each play, after your first visit they keep sending you tons of freebies, as well as invitations for free overnight stays and free buffets.

This happens all the time and will happen even more often if special events occur, such as concerts. For example, let us say you receive an invitation for two free tickets for the Hot August Night concert event in Reno, Nevada, as well as an invitation to play at the slot machine tournament with a certain amount for your buy-in. With the two-day event you are also given a free T-shirt and a bottle of wine. This is a very interesting setup, and sometimes it is hard to past up this kind of offer. You take this invitation and then attend their concert and spend some of your money, and maybe you even win some money in return.

As the gambling industry is becoming more and more competitive, the competition is becoming more intense, and promotions like this are now standard throughout the gambling industry. Casinos actively promote these types of activities to certain age groups or certain kinds of players. Some casinos even offer you a free bus to take you to and from your hometown, if it is not too far from their casino.

High rollers—those who gamble over a hundred dollars a hand for extended periods of time—are especially attractive to casinos. However, if you are a non-aggressive player and play the slot machines or table games with minimum bets, your reward is often just as good as a high roller. After you use my method and win big, some casinos will consider you a high roller and will invite you back to their casinos frequently, with free weekend hotels, free meals, and free coupons to play certain games worth a certain value. Keep in mind that some casinos are more generous than others when it comes to offering promotions.

However, watch out for these freebies if there is a catch to this type of promotion. When you arrive at that casino, you will ask yourself, "Do I need to play heavy to get invited again, or do I just keep my bet to a low point to see where I'm going?"

I would say that you should play with the minimum amount at the beginning and then go up some if the table is performing well for you. You will not be penalized for playing low at the beginning. You must not let the promotion overtake you by making you play foolishly and lose big. You must control your playing without regard to how the casinos keep track of your point systems. Forget about that for a while and play low until you begin to see daylight in the tunnel; then you can afford to play heavy if conditions warrant it. All casinos want to give you some kind of freebie, even if you play low.

These promotions and special offers seem like good deals because it looks like the whole thing is free—except that you must still pay attention to what you are doing in the game table. Make several copies of my forms and use them to keep track of the table to maximize your gambling potential and win some money. Then you will have a completely free trip for the first time.

# PART III:
# PLAY TO WIN

# CHAPTER 12:
## FACING THE CHALLENGE WITH THE HOPE OF FINAL CONQUEST

So far you have mastered my materials, and I hope you will continue using my forms to keep track of all of your game activities. After a long period of data collection, you may wish to compare your data to my outcomes. You may be surprised to learn that both of our data sets are quite similar. The probability curve does not change, but your playing habit has likely changed somewhat due to reading this book.

I have provided you with adequate information and guidance so that you will become a good craps player. You must play this game with the utmost caution, patience, and tolerance. This is a game of chance, and there is no sure thing to win every time. There is no luck for everyone to make money on every hand or game. However, think in turns of your chance at winning this game compared to other casino games. You have a much better opportunity of winning in this game than playing blackjack, for example, because you have better odds by betting the pass line or come out line with full odds. Playing the slot machines is like buying a lottery ticket; the odds of winning are much less than you would have at a craps game. You are doing even better in the craps game if you know how to set the dice and control them before throwing them. There are more and more experts that say controlling and setting the dices before throwing them give you an edge over the house. We will discuss dice control in detail in chapter 15. Random throwing of the dice can give the house a 2 percent advantage over you. This is not much but can tip the scale in the house's favor if you do not follow my rules and using my graphs.

My graphs can guide you in the right direction if play it smart. Pay attention to your accurate recording of the number of throws for each of the six point numbers and record the number of good throws versus the number of bad throws. If you have recorded all activities at a craps table for an extended period of time, your data will show that there are even a number of good hands and bad hands. I suggest you play lightly in this situation; perhaps you should employ the method of waiting for the point number to come out, and then wait for the shooter to throws his second time placing your bets beginning on the third throw. Then follow this for another three rolls and then take down all of your bets. This method is designed to avoid damage from a 7 coming out on every six throws. You can employ this method even if the table has only four players at any given time. If a table has only two players, you should go to another table or wait until you see more players come to play.

This book teaches you how to play under normal conditions. You may also consider playing in the opposite way, so called the house way. Then you will play against the other players at the table. Sometimes it is necessary to do just that. If you see that the game is going nowhere, such as one good hand and then one bad hand, then you should use this approach.

In this situation, you should wait for the shooter to make one point number. At the beginning of the second throwing, you bet the don't pass line with lays. You do not want to bet any more. Play in this way until the table is hot, and then go back to betting in a normal way, the good hand way. But you must keep track of all the activities on every throw and every point number made, and do not let one unrecorded event go by even if someone tries to distract your attention and keep your eyes away from the game.

Keeping accurate records is your only chance to win in the event of a hot hand or break-even hand or a nowhere hand. If you do not record just three counts, the data may not be as useful as you would under normal recording conditions. For example, you may overcount or undercount certain point numbers and make your bets slightly differently. Your outcome could be different, also—you may get the point number bet back, or you may not get back your bets if the 7 comes out. Sometimes you will see someone throws the dice out of the table. The shooter may request for the same dice or may even get a brand-new set of dices and start using them. Under this condition, some players will call for "Off my bets on all numbers," while other players will continue the play as if the dice did not go off the table.

Sometimes you come to a hot table and start playing the game, and you find out that the shooter has already made four point numbers, and some of them are repeat point numbers. You then ask, "Did the shooter make these point numbers by throwing lots of numbers, or just a quick throw and getting his point number?" There is a big difference in each event. If the shooter gets a point number by throwing lots of numbers, without a 7 at the beginning or at any other time, and he can still make that many points numbers, you should play with caution because the probability of throwing a 7 is once every six throws. Chances are that he will throw the 7 at any time. There is no way out for this unfortunate outcome.

On the other hand, if the same shooter shoots four point numbers and makes these numbers in a quick throw two or three times, then you should play heavy while he is throwing the dice. You must take back your bets when he has thrown four or six times without throwing the point number, because this shooter has a habit of throwing short passes and is now out of that habit, which means the hot hand is cooling off. Take special notice—this type of situation occurs quite often.

Playing craps for the first time is a challenge. Please pay special attention to all my reading materials and get accustomed to my graphs and to using my form. You must not go to the tables without taking my form with you. Use that form for all occasions—at Indian casinos, Reno, Atlantic City, and Las Vegas. Do not take shortcuts and eliminate certain sections of this form; each part has a specific purpose. Use this form wisely and correctly because it is the only tool you will ever need to help you get through a rough game and unexpected events.

Now you have the knowledge to face this game's challenges and play this game correctly. All you need to do is get out there and set the stage for your final conquest!

# CHAPTER 13:
## DICE SETTING AND DICE CONTROL

**M**any beginners go to a craps table, arbitrarily pick up two dice, and start throwing them. They do not care which dice they pick. Sometimes the dice will landed outside the table, and other times the dice identically hit someone on the opposite side of the table. In some cases, a few shooters throw the dice just two or three feet from where they are standing. Still other players continue talking to their buddy while throwing the dices. You are not that type of players. You should pay full attention while you are throwing the dices. Your objective is to win quick and to not waste time.

To play craps correctly, you will need to practice how to throw the dices and how to set your dice before throwing them. There are some who will dispute this fact, but many others will tell you that setting up the dices before throwing them will greatly enhance your chance of winning. This kind of throwing is not random, even though the dice are still control by the mathematical probability outcome. Your odds against the house actually increase when you use a dice-control method.

### The Preset Numbers Method

Here we will discuss a main type of shooter, the so-called preset, or preselected numbers, shooter. These types of shooters align the dice in a certain way in their hand before they throw. They know which number is facing every way. For example, one shooter may select a pair of 3 s facing a certain way and then throw the dice to the other side of the table with just enough force to slightly hit the cube rubber and land in a predetermined way. By doing this, the shooter is looking for certain numbers to come out, hoping such the outcome is the point number, or any other number the shooter hopes to get on that throw. Many times in the past, I have seen shooters use the same set of numbers facing certain direction for all their throws. They expect that such throws make many different point numbers, or they may be hoping to get that particular point number or an established point number during the first throw. Some very experienced shooters can make many point numbers by using this system.

For example, in 2009 I was playing at the Paris Casino on a regular weekday. It was Thursday night around 8:24 PM, and I arrived at a table as an older, heavyset gentleman had just thrown his third point number. These three point numbers were identified by certain "fire bet" markers, appearing in three different spots or point numbers on the table. The same shooter could have been or had already made duplicate point numbers before I came to this table. (I later found out that this reselected number shooter had made four point numbers, including one duplicate number, 6.) When I saw this shooter already made these three point numbers (4, 6, and 9), and he started to begin his new throw, a new game, I was anxious to play heavy and placed $10 on the pass line bet before his beginning throw. To start with, he used or lined up certain numbers on the dice. Then he was ready to throw, and he played on the left side of the stickman.

Before he started to throw the dice, he would swing his right hand back and forth a couple times and then threw the dices. This method had not attracted the casino's attention for the time being, but it was very close to it. I later found out that this gentleman was a regular customer for that casino, and that was the main reason for the casino not causing an issue over this preset and controlled throwing. If this same person were playing in another casino, he probably would have received a dirty look from the employees at the table.

To continue with the story, his throw was not far from the end of the table. In fact he was right handed, and it took him just a small distant to throw the dice. Therefore he did not use very much force to make his throws.

I knew then that he was an expert in this type of accurate throwing. Before the throw was made, he looked at the end table to see the distance, so he swung his right hand a couple times carefully, so that the dice would barely hit the end table and bounce out to land at a certain point number. He used this method and threw three times, and then came the point number. This point number was the fourth point number, for fire bet purposes. In fact, this was his fifth point number, because he'd already made a duplicate point number before.

Sometimes he did not quite hit the end table, and the dices did not bounce. The stickman looked at him and did not say anything. Also, he was doing a good job of pleasing the dealers by placing a $5 chip on the table for the dealers to win. And do you know what happened? The boxman was not quite happy with his throw and immediately asked the shooter to hit the dices to the end table with a polite and smiling manner. The shooter nodded his head. Sometimes you can get away by not hitting the end table. If you were to continue this practice, you would not last long at that table because the boxman or the big pit boss would say something bad to you, and then you would take notice and begin to play poorly. So be careful when you throw those dice. Make sure they land or hit the end table, slightly if you can help it.

The large shooter, using some form of practiced dice, used certain numbers to set them in a certain direction or way before throwing them. He had done so many, many times and could hit the end table slightly, and the boxman could not say anything about that throw. In the next two throws, he again made another point number. This was his fifth point number. After that he threw a 10 as his first number. If he was able to duplicate that throw, it would be his sixth point number—the last point number he must make to win his fire bet with a straight set of six point numbers. After that he threw some more numbers, horn number 2 and 11, and then on his fifth throw it was a 7, for a seven-out. He did not make that last point number, but he made five different point numbers. He was very good and very accurate in his throwing. He had won tons of money because he played heavy, and he was a shooter by his own right. He deserved such an honorable performance, and his name shall be remembered for a long time.

Because the shooter had placed $5 for his fire bet at the beginning, his return was $5 times $500, which was equal to $2,500. This was his extra money he made because of his skills and accuracy and using the predetermined numbers for all his throws. After the 7 came out before another point number, this shooter cashed out and left. He was happy, smiled, and gracefully walked away from the table. He also gave $25 to the dealers for their patience and kindness. There were other players who also cashed out and left. After some of these players left, there were only five that remained. The new shooter was in line to play the next game. This new shooter threw and established a point number, and he continued to throw three more times before a 7 came. Then came the next player. This player also threw a new point number on the first throw. After four times or four throws, the 7 came out for seven-out again. I left the table and cashed my money in. In this late arrival to the table, I was able to profit in excess of over $200. Other players still stayed at the same table even after such a hot hand. But you should remember that after a hot hand, you must make plans to exit the table at the end of the throw or on the next seven-out.

Dice setting or controlled throwing is an old method and has been in used for a long time. Although many experts strongly believe this to be a waste of time, I am content that this is the best way to play this game and win big dollars. I have researched this area for some time and believe that you have a good edge over the house if you select the right combination of dice numbers, set them in a proper way, and throw with a certain strength to get them to land in a certain way. This method is much better than just randomly throwing. You will now learn the basics of this method, but you must promise me that you will not use these strategies at the table until you have fully mastered them, and until you have a complete confidence in yourself.

Readers who have strong interest in perfecting this dice control method should consider buying the following two books: *The Golden Touch Dice*

*Control Revolution* by Frank Scoblete, and *Dominator and Wong on Dice* by Stanford Wong. These books can teach you the basics, but the rest will depend on how much effort you put in to practice by using their techniques.

# Setting the Dice

Controlled dice throwing involves many components. First, though, you must set the dice in a certain way, with certain numbers on the top and certain numbers on the bottom. How you set the dices will affect the outcome of the throw. One of the most popular sets is the 3-V pattern, in which you set the 3s in a "V" formation. The bottom numbers must be the same every time you set them. When you throw the dice, this will give you hard 6 on the top and regular 6 on the front, an 8 on one side and on the back side, and the hard 8 on the bottom. There are no sevens showing on the dice with this set.

I have come across three good ways to set the dice in a controlled manner. Of course there are many other variations, but I feel that you should only concentrate on these three settings and practice them until you feel comfortable to use them for your throwing purposes. Remember, the purpose of setting the dices in a precise location is to try to get a predetermined point number that you are seeking or betting to come out before the 7 comes.

The three good ways to hold the dices are as follows.

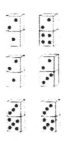

**Note: The top number is facing the top, while the bottom number is facing the shooter.**

The first throw would get points 4, 5, 9, and 10.

The second throw would get points 4 and 10.

The third throw would get hard numbers: 4, 6, 8, and 10.

When you set the dice, you must set them quickly, otherwise you will hear the stickman or the boxman say something like, "Please throw the dice." If that happens, you will get upset and may become too nervous; then your new technique will become the old technique of throwing unexpectedly and landing a number you do not want. Be prepared and do your setting fast. Before you receive your dice, you should be thinking in turns of what number you need to line up on the left and on the right. When you do receive them, you must act quickly and efficiently to set the dices and start planning to throw.

Once you have a plan as how you want to line up the dices, how much pressure do you need, and how many fingers to use to hold them, then you need to know how to deliver them to other end of the table and be successful at landing the point number you desire.

# Throwing the Dice

In a controlled throwing, you must ask yourself, "How many fingers do I need to control my dice before throwing them?" You may use two specific fingers or three fingers or five fingers to begin your practice, but you must use the same method every time.

There are basically three areas of concern: the way you grip the dice, how you align the dice, and how you deliver them to the end of the table without throwing them over the board or allowing them to bounce randomly.

The secret to this is to achieve backspin while making sure that the dice do not move on any other axes. If properly delivered, the dice will stay together as they fly through the air, rotating only on the right-left axes.

When you throw these dice, you must use a smooth delivery so that the dice hit the other side of the table and bounce with just enough force to land on your desired number. If you fail to bounce the dices, you will be notified by the stickman right away. You also want to make sure you use the exact force and pattern in your subsequent throws. Throwing the same way every time is very hard, and it takes a lot of practice before you can claim it as a success.

This dice setting method is sometimes called rhythm rolling. In many cases and at a hot table, many craps players have witnessed a hot roll as the shooter threw numbers after numbers. This may occur over fifteen times without a 7 coming out. By throwing the dice in the same manner each time, some shooters get into a rhythm that has produced monstrous rolls. For some shooters who have not perfected such a throw, the outcome is very poor, and 7s come out quite quickly. Some shooters who try to practice rhythm rolling do this consciously, but others are unaware that they are doing it.

There is no difference if you are left handed or right handed. Age and gender are not a factor, and neither is where you stand to throw the dice. You must simply take enough practice to perfect your technique. I suggest practicing the set dice throwing at home for at least few months to get a smooth and consistent throw to achieve a perfect throwing technique.

# Rules for Practice

There are certain points that you must know before using this technique. You must not overuse your technique, and do not let people know that you have acquired this special method. You should play this game as naturally as possible; do not show off and talk to your neighbor about how you just learned this and are going to make a killing. Do not bet heavy at first, and do not buy into the table with a large sum. Just focus on your technique and have fun.

The following are some methods to use as you improve your delivery system.

1. Be sure to watch out for your thumb when tossing the dice. Both dice should be thrown at the same time.

2. Backspin is placed on the dice to counter the forward motion of the dices and to keep them from landing on a random number after bouncing against the back wall of the table.

3. Sweaty fingers can also become a problem when tossing the dice. If you have such a problem, carry chalk in your pocket and use it.

4. When you throw the dice, they should rotate together in the air, their left and right axes should be parallel to the table, and they should bounce straight forward.

5. When tossing the dice, try and make them look like a natural throw. Do not try to tip the dices back and forth to look for the bottom numbers or side numbers.

Now you have learned some basic facts on controlled dice throwing. With practice you will gain confidence in your throwing and will become a precision shooter in no time. Then all you have to do is walk up to a craps table and wait for your turn to throw!

# CHAPTER 14:
# RULES TO FOLLOW

Throughout my thirty years playing craps, I have developed certain methods or rules to use in my game. Use my rules freely, but you also should develop your own and see if they are working. If your method is not working, perhaps you have not followed same basic rules. Maybe you are too aggressive in your playing habit. Maybe you are not paying attention to the surrounding conditions to see if this is a hot or cold table. You may be in a hurry to jump in and start playing the game without further investigation as to how well everyone is doing in the table. Your urge to play in a hurry will bring you no profit in return. You have lots of time to play this game correctly in an eight-hour environment. Be kind to yourself and slow down.

I have developed the following criteria for you to consider. You should adopt some of or all of these rules, because they will greatly improve your winning hands.

1. Pay attention to a table filled with: mature players with lots of $25 chips, chips stretching out over one foot long, people who are happy and cheerful, and players giving large tips to the shooter and to the dealers. You should get in and start playing. But remember, play to win a small sum and exit the table if needed.

2. When you play a Harrah's-owned casino, such as Flamingo Casino, Paris Casino, Bally Casino, PH Casino, Harrah's Las Vegas Casino, and

Harrah's Reno Casino, they have a system called "fire bet" to keep track of how many of the point numbers have already been thrown by the same shooter. But this fire bet indicator does not tell the whole story, because the shooter may have already thrown the same point numbers twice before or more than once for the same point number. To play the fire bet, at the beginning of the new game you can place $1–5 in front of your number on the table, just below your sitting. When the shooter rolls four different point numbers, such as 4, 5, 6, and 8, and a 7 out before another point number comes out, you still win $25 for your fire bet of $1 because you hit four of the six point numbers.

For you to start playing in this hot hand environment, when you come to this table for the first time and see that there are two or three fire bet numbers already out, and these fire bet indicators show on the point number, you should pay some attention to that table, especially when the shooter makes a quick strike, such as two to four throws for another point number to come out before a 7 does. If he can do that, you should go in and start playing right away. But remember, if the shooter throws another point number, such 10, and he continues to throw several times without hitting that point number, then you should plan for an exit strategy because the shooter is certainly not going to make that point; he can make point number in a short hub and cannot make point numbers in a long roll of throwing dices.

3. When you start playing in a table, and a shooter throws two or three times and makes a point number, and then on the next throw, she throws another point number, throws two to three times, then makes that point number, and continues doing that—then you should increase your betting to heavy at certain points and be prepared to exit if she throws beyond five to seven times without making that point number. She has made a habit of short number passes and cannot do well in long throw passes.

4. Look for a table with built-in solid chains were many shooters continuously and consistently make point numbers without any bad hands between them. If the fifth shooter makes one or two point numbers, then

you should bet heavy beginning on your sixth shooter, at the beginning of a new game, because this chain is very solid and cannot be broken until you see or pass beyond the eighth shooter. If the sixth shooter could not make the point number, please do not be discouraged because this can happen once in awhile. The next shooter, will definitely make another point number to make up the money you lost with shooter six, and you can still make up a solid chain as I have pointed before. After the number seven shooter makes a point number, such as a one- or two-point number, you should play maybe just one more hand and be prepared to exit from that table as soon as you see another 7 out before making another point. This is the best table and the best chance to win big. Be prepared for this kind of hot and solid chain table, because they do not come very often.

5. Do not play at a table filled with young people who are drinking and shouting to each other. Do not play at a table where a shooter moves with the dice back and forth before throwing them. This is a random throw, and you do not want that to happen.

6. Do not play at a table with just one or two players, or with each player having little or no chips left. Go away unless you want to gamble at your own risk.

8. Do not play at a table with lots of players arguing over certain payoffs; some can go overboard and get mad and shout dirty words.

9. Keep track of the exact number of good hands versus bad hands. Pay attention to a table where you may encounter shooters who consistently make point numbers and continue throwing lots of numbers before seven-out. This is a long roll shooter and is hard to find. Pay close attention to this kind of throw, especially if this shooter has already thrown eleven times and consistently makes number after numbers.

10. Keep track of these six points numbers and see which come out the most and which come out the least. Pay special attention to those point

numbers that come out much less than normal, and pay heavy on those numbers. You should perform a periodic calculation to see which numbers are under or over the probability average. Concentrate on the underthrown numbers, and you will see how beneficial this tool is for you just by paying attention to this particular area.

11. You should employ a new method of betting on this game. This is called the gold chain strategy. It is very simple to use and yet may make you good money in the short term. To begin with, you should let the shooter make a point number first. At the beginning of the third throw, you place your bets on the field and then place bets on 5, 6, and 8, for a total of four different bets. If the next throw is 5, you will gain by betting on the 5, but you lose on the field. You will take the profit from the 5 and use that to bet on the field again. If you gain a certain amount and continue doing this until the same shooter has already thrown six or seven times, from this point on please be cautious and prudent and thrifty. Try to take down all of the bets, because for every six throws there will be a 7 coming out.

This method has some drawbacks because if you place a field bet and the number comes out a 5, for example, you will gain $2 from this hand. If the next number is 6, you will gain just $1. This process will take a long time to earn a decent living. What I am proposing is this: Use this method on the very hot hand or solid chain environment, by going heavy in these bets. On the other hand, if the same shooter is still shooting after eleven throws, you could continue betting by using the same method but with a reduced size of your bets until the 7 comes out. By doing this you already made your profits by betting heavy at the beginning, and you can afford to lose some later on.

12. You should play the don't pass line when you see one shooter shoot lots of number and then get his point number. If he does this continuously without any 7 coming out, or he comes out on the first throw and gets his next point number, then you should concentrate playing the don't pass and be happy with the outcome. You have an edge over the shooter because he throws many, many numbers with no 7 coming out. The possibility

of a 7 coming out in the future is much greater than getting another point number. You have a much greater advantage, and that is the house advantage.

Try to test these methods individually or collectively to see which of them will work for you. You must be patient as you begin to use my methods for the very first time. Once you master the system, then you can relax and use any appropriate method in your system to enhance your chances of winning. At the same time, you must prepare for losing some. Do not build up too much expectation or excessive greed. Play with style and winning will be your game.

# CHAPTER 15:
# THE FINAL GAME PLAN

To win in game requires certain skill. You cannot solely depend on someone who can shoot point numbers for you, and you cannot shoot any point numbers for them. You must contribute your full effort for the benefit of all. As such, you should learn how to throw the dice well and make point numbers for everyone.

The craps game is an exciting and rewarding adventure, and you can hear people shouting and yelling. There are not too many games in a casino that will bring you this type of enjoyment. No other casino game gives you these odds for your money, if you place a maximum-odds for your pass line and come out line bets. This game can be played in a normal way or in the opposite, house way: pass line, or don't pass line. Either way is an acceptable method. If you see the few previous shooters made point numbers, then it is good for you to play the pass line at the beginning. If you see that no previous shooters could make point numbers, or four or five shooters missed, then it is best for you to play the don't pass line at the beginning of the game. It may seem like this is a very complex matter, but really the winning strategy is simple and requires no long-term memory.

You must first keep track of all point numbers, one at a time, from shooter one to shooter fifteen, for example. You must record all fifteen times how many shooters make one, two, three, and four point numbers. Record these in the proper columns of your form. As soon as you record a shooter already made three point numbers, you should play heavy on the next play: Play the don't pass line, and place a certain amount on the 7 also to cover in case of it comes out first. Then lay the full amount on the don't bet line. As you can see, there is only a 3.8 percent chance for the shooter to shoot 4 point numbers. If you make this money by playing don't pass, you should wait for another chance or walk away for good.

If you lost this bet because the shooter throws another point number, his fourth, do not be discouraged because this can happen once in a while. But remember, he was lucky because his chance of throwing the point number was only 3.8 percent, and your chance was almost 96 percent. You have the much better odds.

So what do you do from this point on? Stay put and wait for the next opportunity. In the meanwhile, play with just a small sum of money to keep you busy. You do not have to play if you wish to wait for your opportunity. When you see another shooter throw three point numbers later, you should recoup your loss by betting the amount you lost last time, plus the new game's amount that you can afford. You may bet at the beginning of the new throw or wait until a new number came out first. Perhaps a better method is to buy a lay for the fourth established point number. In my thirty years of gambling, I have seen, on average, four point numbers occur two times in any given day, in six hours of playing. You should concentrate all your effort in this area if no other areas have given you satisfaction. From that point on, you should be able to recoup all of your investments. This is your best chance to win.

Now you have all the knowledge that you need to go out and play craps well and win. But you must also remember that a wise man once said that it is better to take a minor beating than to lose one's fortune. To be success in this game, you must learn how to play it well and place your bets well. Good luck to you and to your future fortune!